INSTANT POT COOK-BOOK FOR BEGINNERS

INSTANT POT COOK-BOOK FOR BEGINNERS

THE ESSENTIAL GUIDE TO YOUR ELECTRIC PRESSURE COOKER

Lauren Keating

Photography by Darren Muir

ROCKRIDGE
PRESS

For general information on our other products and services or to obtain technical support, please contact our Customer Care Department within the United States at (866) 744-2665, or outside the United States at (510) 253-0500.

Rockridge Press publishes its books in a variety of electronic and print formats. Some content that appears in print may not be available in electronic books, and vice versa.

Interior and Cover Designer: Richard Tapp
Art Producer: Sue Bischofberger
Editor: Justin Hartung
Production Editor: Emily Sheehan

Production Manager: Michael Kay

Photography © 2021 Darren Muir; food styling by Yolanda Muirc. Author photo courtesy of Lana Ortiz.

Cover: Spaghetti and Meatballs, page 75.

ISBN: Print 978-1-64876-995-5
eBook 978-1-64876-996-2

R0

To Shawn:
Thanks for always being my number-one fan and
for encouraging my experiments in the kitchen.

Contents

Introduction

I'm going to let you in on a little secret: I don't always love cooking.

Sure, making a new recipe can be fun on a lazy Sunday afternoon when there isn't anything else going on. But on a Monday after a busy day at work? I'd rather skip straight to the eating part of the night.

I think that's why I love kitchen gadgets so much. Modern kitchen appliances can help get dinner on the table faster and with less effort—plus all of those buttons and lights can make cooking a little more fun when you don't really feel like doing it.

When I bought my first Instant Pot a few years ago, I was really excited about the prospect of a seemingly space-age gadget that promised to shave valuable time off the cooking process. I eagerly opened the box and then, like so many other people, I put the whole thing in the closet and didn't touch it for months.

As a cooking school graduate, I had a ton of experience cooking on the stove top and with a slow cooker. But the Instant Pot looked like it was dropped onto my counter from another planet. I had no idea where to even start. Coupled with

stories of exploding stovetop pressure cookers that shot spaghetti sauce onto the ceiling, I'll admit that I was intimidated.

I'm a researcher by nature, so I started reading books cover to cover and saved every article I could find about pressure cooking. I quickly learned the science of pressure cooking and was reassured that electric pressure cookers are much safer and more user-friendly than the stovetop versions our grandparents used. I also learned that, while Instant Pots look complicated, most of the buttons are just presets to help you make common items with just one touch.

I finally pulled mine back out of the closet and made chicken burrito bowls. They were ready in about a half hour—less time than it would have taken me to get takeout and tastier, too! The next night, I made a spicy vegetarian curry. Then I used my Instant Pot to turn leftover roast chicken into the most delicious homemade stock I had ever tasted.

I was officially hooked.

That's not to say everything came out perfectly right from the start. I had my fair share of recipe mishaps, most due to user error. But now using my Instant Pot is second nature, and I don't think twice before using it to make an easy and delicious meal. I included several Instant Pot recipes in my first cookbook and have shared others on my blog, Healthy-Delicious.com, as well as on other websites across the internet.

In this book, I'll walk you through the basics of using your Instant Pot so that you can avoid common mistakes and start churning out perfect recipes right away.

In the first chapter, I'll teach you everything you need to know about your new kitchen appliance—from what all of those buttons do to how to wash it to what to do if things don't seem to be working out properly. I know it's tempting to skip this chapter and dive right into the recipes, but I encourage you to read it thoroughly and refer to it often. In the long run, it might save you a lot of frustration.

Once we've tackled the basics, I'll walk you through 80 tasty recipes that I just know you and your family will love. They're the kind of down-home comfort food recipes that feel like a warm hug after a long day. And they're all written with beginners in mind.

It's my hope that this book will help you use your Instant Pot confidently and will set you up for success in the kitchen.

Happy cooking!

CHAPTER 1

Instant Pot 101

Welcome to the Instant Pot family! You're officially one step closer to getting delicious meals on the table quickly and easily. But what exactly is this thing, and how do you use it?

If you've picked up this book before buying an Instant Pot, this chapter will go over the basics of how electric pressure cookers work, how to use them to get the best results, and what to do if things go wrong. We'll also break down the different models that are available. Read this chapter thoroughly and refer back to it often. You'll be a pro in no time!

THE INSTANT POT AND HOW IT WORKS

So, you bought an Instant Pot or, even better, received one as a gift. What now? Before you dive right in to cooking your favorite meal, it can be helpful to get a basic understanding of what pressure cooking is and how it works. You'll also want to get acquainted with your pot and learn the nuances of the specific model and size that you'll be cooking with. If you haven't purchased a pot yet, this will help you decide which one is best for you and your family.

Models and Sizes

There are currently no fewer than 13 Instant Pot models available in stores. Some have additional bells and whistles like built-in Wi-Fi, air fryer lids, or sous vide functions, but all of them have basic pressure cooking abilities.

Each model also comes in several different size options. The most common size is the 6-quart version. This is considered standard and is the size that most Instant Pot recipes are written for. It's perfect for families of four or five people or for couples who love leftovers.

If you have a larger family or like to cook for a crowd, the 8-quart model might be more your speed. If you like to host parties or are big on cooking ahead and stocking the freezer, the Duo Nova is available in a massive 10-quart option.

A 3-quart model is available if you're cooking for one or have very limited space, but note that it has fewer features than the larger models.

ADJUSTING RECIPES FOR VARIOUS INSTANT POT SIZES

The recipes in this book were all developed using a 6-quart Instant Pot. If yours is larger or smaller, that's okay, but you'll need to make some adjustments.

If you have a 3-quart Instant Pot, cut the amount of each ingredient in half. Be sure to use the minimum amount of liquid (½ cup).

Many of the recipes in this book can be made in an 8-quart Instant Pot without any adjustments. As long as the original recipe includes at least 2 cups of liquid, you're good to go. If the recipe has less liquid than that, you'll need to scale it up; most recipes can be doubled without any issues.

If a recipe uses the pot-in-pot cooking technique or if the liquid is only used to make steam and doesn't come into contact with the ingredients, like the Ham-and-Cheese Omelet (page 18) or Fudgy Brownie Bites (page 126), you can keep the recipe as is and simply increase the amount of water to 2 cups.

No matter what size Instant Pot you have, be sure to keep an eye on the Max Fill line and remember that you only need to adjust the ingredient amounts; the cooking time will stay the same.

Cooking Under Pressure

Pressure cooking has risen in popularity over the past few years, but this method of cooking dates back to the 1600s. Pressure cookers have taken many shapes and forms over the years, and the invention of modern electric pressure cookers like the Instant Pot makes the process easier than ever!

Pressure cookers are airtight pots that rely on liquid, such as water or broth, to create steam. Since the steam has no way of escaping, it creates a high-pressure environment inside the pot and increases the boiling point of water from 212°F to 250°F. This higher temperature means food cooks about 30 percent faster than it would on the stove top. Since the closed cooking environment prevents evaporation, the food also retains more moisture and flavor.

FIVE REASONS YOU'RE GOING TO LOVE YOUR INSTANT POT

Have you ever noticed how Instant Pot fans can't seem to stop talking about them? Indeed, there are so many things about them to love. Here are a few of the top reasons you'll fall in love with yours.

1. **It saves you time.** It's so easy to throw a few ingredients into the Instant Pot and have a delicious dinner, even if you don't plan ahead. You can add meat right from the freezer and still have dinner on the table in under an hour with minimal effort. Gone are the days of needing to commit to an entire afternoon at home to make a fall-apart pot roast or tender stew.

2. **It makes cleanup easy.** Thanks to the Instant Pot's sauté feature, you can brown meat and soften vegetables right in the same pot before turning the pressure on. That means one less pot to wash! Plus, the inner pot itself cleans up easily and is dishwasher safe.

3. **It makes food taste better.** Since liquids don't evaporate like they do with traditional cooking methods, no flavor is lost. This means flavors are more intense and seasonings infuse foods better. You'll love how broths and sauces taste like they've simmered all day.

4. **It's for more than just dinner.** While quick-and-easy dinners are what draw most people to electric pressure cookers, you can also use them to make breakfasts and desserts. You can even use your Instant Pot to make homemade yogurt or steam vegetables!

5. **It's fun!** Cooking night after night can feel like a chore, but having a new kitchen gadget like an Instant Pot can make it fun again. Taking the lid off at the end of the cooking process and seeing how the raw ingredients transformed into a complete meal can seem like magic. And no matter how many times you use the Instant Pot, watching the jet of steam escape during a quick release never gets old.

INSTANT POT COMPONENTS

In addition to the base unit and lid, your Instant Pot comes with several other important components. These include the inner pot, the condensation collector, and a metal trivet. Depending on the model of your unit, the power cord might arrive detached, and there might be some other accessories included, like a measuring cup or spoons.

As outlined in the following paragraphs, a few components need special care that might not be obvious right away.

Inner Pot

For most recipes, food will cook directly inside the inner pot. This stainless steel pot is removable and can be washed in the dishwasher for easy cleanup. Always double-check to make sure the pot has been returned to the base unit before adding your recipe ingredients; you should never place food directly into the base.

Sealing Ring

The silicone sealing ring is a very important part of your Instant Pot. Without it, steam will escape, and the pot won't come to pressure. To remove the ring after cooking, gently pull it until it slips out from behind the wire holding it in place. You can wash the sealing ring in the top rack of your dishwasher or by hand. When replacing the ring, be sure to push it in firmly and make sure no pieces are sticking out from behind the wire. The sealing ring can stretch out and dry out over time, preventing your pot from getting a tight seal. Replacements are very affordable, and it's not a bad idea to have an extra on hand. Some people also like to use one ring for savory foods and another for sweets, since the silicone can absorb some flavors.

Steam Valve

This valve, located on the pot's lid, regulates the pressure inside the pot. It should be cleaned periodically, especially after cooking starchy or highly fragrant foods. To remove the valve, take off the small silicone cap on the underside of the pot lid. Once the cap is removed, the valve should slip freely through the hole on the top of the lid. Wash the valve and cap with a soft brush; then replace both pieces.

Condensation Collector

This is a small, clear cup that attaches to the back of your Instant Pot and collects any moisture that builds up on the pot rim. This can happen during the cooking process or if the lid is propped open. Remove this cup by sliding it straight out and empty it before putting your Instant Pot away. It can be washed by hand or on the top rack of your dishwasher and should easily slide back into place.

KNOW YOUR INSTANT POT

The first step to getting confident with your Instant Pot is to familiarize yourself with all of its buttons and functions. Before making your first recipe in your Instant Pot, it can be helpful to start with a water test (basically just "cooking" 3 cups of water under high pressure for 3 minutes) so that you can get a feel for how everything works and how much time each step takes.

Following is a general overview of the basics to get you started, but the exact buttons your pot has will depend on its size and model.

Start

If you have an Instant Pot Ultra, Duo Evo Plus, or Max, your pot will have a Start button. In this case, you'll need to press this button to turn your Instant Pot on. If your model doesn't have a start button, don't worry! The pot will turn on automatically when you press a function button or set the timer.

Keep Warm

If you don't plan to eat your meal right away, pressing the Keep Warm button will keep your cooked food at a safe temperature for up to 10 hours. You can enable this feature at the beginning of the cooking process or at any time after the process has started. If this button is pressed before the cooking process starts, it will begin counting up once the cooking cycle is complete and will not turn off until you hit Cancel or 10 hours have gone by. This is helpful for keeping track of how long pressure has been naturally releasing. If the Keep Warm button is pressed after the cooking cycle has completed, it will default to 10 hours. You can increase or reduce this time by pressing the +/- buttons.

Cancel

You can stop any function by hitting the Cancel button. Note that on older models, this button is combined with the Keep Warm button. To completely cut off power to the device, you should unplug it.

Sauté

One of the most exciting features of the Instant Pot is that you can also use it to sauté or brown food right in the same pot before cooking it under pressure. To do this, press the Sauté button and give the pot about a minute to heat up before adding your food. Depending on your model, press Sauté again to increase or reduce the heat level as necessary. When you're done, press Cancel. It is not necessary to use a lid when using the sauté function.

Pressure Cook

For pressure cooking, you'll need to decide if you want to use one of the preset buttons or adjust the pressure and time manually. The recipes in this book all use manual settings to give you the most control over the cooking process, but the preset buttons can be very convenient, too. Do note that there are some differences here between older and newer models.

MANUAL

Start by pressing the Pressure Cook button. If the pressure level needs to be adjusted, hit the Pressure Level button to toggle between the high and low options. Most recipes use high pressure, but low pressure is useful for cooking delicate vegetables or for making rice. Finally, press the +/- buttons to adjust the timer. Press the Start button if your pot has one. If it doesn't, the pot will turn on automatically. Be patient; it will take about 10 seconds for this to happen. The pot will beep several times to indicate that the cooking process has started.

PRESETS

Depending on the model Instant Pot you have, there will also be several preset buttons that are programmed with appropriate pressure and time settings for common recipes. Keep in mind that your Instant Pot doesn't know exactly what you put in it, so these presets are based on average cook times. You'll need to test your food when the time is up to make sure it's done. You can also use the +/- buttons to increase or decrease the preset cooking time, as appropriate.

Commonly used preset buttons include:

Soup/Broth: For making brothy soups. For meatless soups, use the -button to reduce the cooking time.

Meat/Stew: For bigger pieces of meat or thick stews. The default setting is high pressure for 20 minutes.

Bean/Chili: For dried beans. The default setting is high pressure for 30 minutes, which will result in medium-soft beans.

Poultry: For cooking small, bite-size pieces of boneless chicken. The default setting is high pressure for 12 minutes.

Rice: For cooking white or jasmine rice. The default setting is low pressure for 12 minutes.

Multigrain: For brown rice and tougher whole grains. This setting has a built-in soaking time before the cooking process starts to help grains soften. The default setting is 45 minutes of soaking time followed by 40 minutes of cooking under high pressure.

Porridge: For making rice porridge. The default setting is high pressure for 20 minutes. For oatmeal, use the - button to reduce the cooking time.

Steam: For steaming fish or vegetables. Be sure to insert the steam rack to elevate the food over the cooking liquid and away from the heating element when using this setting. The default setting is high pressure for 10 minutes.

Slow Cook

When you aren't in a hurry, your Instant Pot can double as a slow cooker. Hit Slow Cook and then press Slow Cook again to toggle through heat level options. Normal is equivalent to low heat, More is equivalent to high heat, and Less is equivalent to the Keep Warm setting. Once the appropriate heat level is selected, use the +/- buttons to manually set the timer. Place the lid on the pot, but do not lock or seal it. Alternatively, you can purchase a see-through glass lid.

Yogurt

The Yogurt button can be used to make yogurt by heating milk and then holding it at a steady temperature while it ferments.

Delay Start

The Delay Start button can be used if you don't want to start the pressure cooking process right away. To use this function, choose your pressure cook settings and then press the Delay Start button. Use the +/- buttons to set the timer. Pressure will begin to build once the time has expired. This is useful for doing things like soaking dried beans, but keep in mind that it does not keep uncooked meat at a safe temperature.

IF YOU HAVE AN OLDER MODEL

While the basic functionality of Instant Pots hasn't changed since they were initially released, the design has undergone some updates. If your Instant Pot is an older model, the buttons might look a little different than those described here. The main difference is that older models include Adjust and Manual buttons. Use the Adjust button to toggle between heat options when using the Sauté and Slow Cook functions. You can also press this button to increase or reduce the cook times when using the presets. If your pot includes a Manual button, you'll need to press this before selecting your pressure level and setting the timer if you aren't using one of the pressure cooking presets.

COOKING WITH THE INSTANT POT FOR THE FIRST TIME

Ready to cook in your Instant Pot for the first time? Here's a step-by-step overview of the process that you'll need to follow.

1. **If you want to precook or brown some ingredients, press Sauté.** Press the +/- buttons to increase or decrease the heat level; then give the pot a minute to heat up. Add your ingredients and cook as desired. When you're done, hit Cancel.

2. **Add the remaining ingredients to the pot.** Add the rest of your ingredients to the pot in the order that they're listed in the recipe. Be sure to note whether you should stir them together, as some ingredients will burn if they're too close to the heating element on the bottom of the pot. For proper operation and to prevent the steam valve from clogging, be sure not to overfill the pot. Look for the Max Fill line, indicated two-thirds of the way up the inside of the inner pot.

3. **Make sure the sealing ring is in its proper position inside the lid.** Check your sealing ring to make sure it's attached securely, with the metal wire sitting firmly in the groove of the ring. This is important—if the sealing ring isn't on properly, the pot will not come to pressure.

4. **Lock the lid.** Place the lid on the pot and twist it a quarter turn to the left. The Instant Pot will chime to let you know the lid has been locked in place properly.

5. **Make sure the steam valve is in the Sealing position.** Check the valve on the top of the lid to make sure it's switched to the Sealing position. Depending on the model pot you have, you will need to either rotate the Steam Release switch toward the back of the pot or press the Steam Release button down to ensure the pot is set to Sealing. If the valve is set to Venting, the pot will not come to pressure.

6. **Program the pot.** Set the pressure level and cook time manually or use one of the preset buttons, as described in the previous section. Remember that if your pot has a Start button, you'll need to press it before the cooking process begins. For models without a Start button, the pot will beep to indicate that it is beginning to heat up.

7. **Wait for the pot to come to pressure.** While the pressure inside the pot starts to build, it won't look like anything is happening. The timer will not start counting down until pressure has been established. This process can take 5 to 20 minutes, depending on how much liquid is in the pot and if you started with warm or cold ingredients. Recipes that use a minimal amount of water will achieve pressure quickly, while very full pots or pots that include frozen ingredients will take longer. A minute or so before the pot reaches pressure, you may hear a hissing sound or see some steam escaping from the valve. That's okay! The valve pin will also start to rattle and will pop up and lock the lid in place when pressure has been reached. At this point, the pot will beep, and the timer will start to count down.

8. **Wait for your food to cook.** This is when the magic happens! The timer will begin to count down as your food cooks. Once the time has expired, the pot will beep and switch to Keep Warm. At this point, the timer will start to count up to indicate how long the cooked food has been inside the pot.

9. **Release the pressure.** You will not be able to remove the lid until the pressure has been released. There are two ways to do this: quick release and natural release. Once the pressure has been released, remove the lid carefully by twisting it to the right and then lifting it off. The contents of the pot will still be very hot and steamy, so it's best to open the lid away from your face.

    → **Quick Release:** Quick release lets the pressure out very quickly, typically in less than 1 minute. It's used for cooking things like vegetables, where you want to avoid overcooking. To perform a quick release, switch the valve from the Sealing posting to Venting. Stand back—hot steam will immediately begin to shoot through the valve. You should not perform a quick release if the pot is underneath a cabinet, since the steam can damage it.

    → **Natural Release:** Natural release is a slower process that allows the pressure to release slowly. Use this option for starchy recipes and meats, and keep in mind that whatever is in the pot will continue to cook during this time. The pot will automatically begin to release pressure naturally when the cooking time has expired; you don't need to do anything. Some people like to hit Cancel and turn the pot off at this point, but leaving it on the Keep Warm setting doesn't affect the pot's ability to release pressure and has the added benefit of keeping the timer running so that you can see how long the pressure has been releasing. Just like when pressure is building, it won't look like anything is happening at this point, and there isn't a telltale jet of steam to indicate that pressure is releasing. The process can take 5 to 30 minutes, depending on how much liquid is inside the pot. Recipes with more liquid will take more time to cool and depressurize. You will know that the pressure has dissipated when the float valve drops. At this point, the lid will unlock, and you'll be able to remove it easily.

10. **Finish your recipe.** Taste your creation and adjust the seasoning to your liking. Some recipes may also call for additional ingredients to be added at this point or may instruct you to use the Sauté feature again to bring liquids to a boil and help them reduce.

INSTANT POT SAFETY TIPS

Electric pressure cookers are very safe, but there are some standard precautions that you should take.

Set the pot on a sturdy surface. Be sure to always place your Instant Pot on a study, flat surface and keep it away from the edge of the counter. Don't overstretch the power cord or put it where someone might trip over it. A falling Instant Pot is a recipe for a major mess! Also avoid placing the Instant Pot on the stove. I've heard so many stories about people who accidentally turned the burner on and melted the bottom of their pot.

Maintain your sealing ring. If the sealing ring is not in proper condition or if it's not positioned properly, steam can escape from under the lid, and the pot will not come to pressure. Check your ring before cooking and be sure it doesn't have any cracks, which can occur as it dries out. Rings should be replaced every year or two.

Do not overfill. Be sure to pay attention to the Max Fill line indicated on the inside of the inner pot, especially when doubling a recipe. When cooking starchy ingredients like beans, grains, or pasta, don't fill the pot more than halfway. Remember, food expands when it cooks. If the pot is overfilled, hot ingredients could spill out when the lid is removed. Additionally, starchy ingredients can create hot foam inside the pot that, when overfull, can shoot through the steam valve when releasing pressure.

Stay away from the steam. Always use an oven mitt when switching the valve to Venting, and keep your face away from the pot. Similarly, always open the lid facing away from you so that you don't end up with a face full of hot steam.

Instant Pots have a built-in feature that prevents them from overheating and will automatically turn the appliance off if it detects a risk of food burning. If your Instant Pot shuts itself off before coming to pressure, this is likely what happened. Unplug it, and check to make sure there isn't any food stuck to the bottom of the inner pot, that there's enough liquid, and that the pot was inserted properly. If everything looks okay, you can plug the Instant Pot back in and reprogram the cooking cycle.

MAKING THE MOST OF YOUR INSTANT POT

You'll be able to prepare tons of delicious recipes with your Instant Pot straight from the box, but a few extra accessories will really help you take things to the next level and improve the versatility of your pot.

Here are a few of my favorites:

Trivet

Many recipes make use of a trivet to keep ingredients out of the cooking liquid. Your Instant Pot will come with a metal trivet, but replacing it with a sturdier one can be useful. I personally prefer trivets with long handles, which make it much easier to remove large cuts of meat or baking pans from the pot.

Baking Pans

Speaking of baking pans, these can be used for pot-in-pot cooking and allow you to make baked goods like Chocolate Chip Banana Bread (page 120) in your Instant Pot! You'll need pans that are small enough to fit inside the inner pot easily. Round pans 6 and 7 inches wide are perfect for 6-quart Instant Pots. Pans that are 6 inches wide will also fit inside 3-quart models. A selection of cake pans, Bundt pans, and springform pans can be handy.

Steamer Basket

Steamer baskets are similar to trivets but have higher sides and are made from mesh, so small items won't fall through. They make it easy to remove loose items like baked potatoes and hard-boiled eggs from the pot.

Silicone Egg Bite Molds

These silicone molds are available in 7-cup and 4-cup models, designed to fit inside 6-quart and 3-quart Instant Pot models, respectively. They're great for making egg bites but can also be used to make muffins, pancakes, and even brownies!

Nonstick Insert

If you make a lot of creamy recipes or use the Sauté function often, it can be worth picking up a ceramic-coated insert. This helps prevent food from sticking to the bottom of the inner pot, helping you avoid a burn warning and making cleanup even easier.

Glass Lid

If you like to use your Instant Pot as a slow cooker or to simmer recipes or keep them warm, you may want to consider purchasing a clear glass lid with a steam vent. Note that these lids cannot be used while pressure cooking.

Air Fryer Lid

If you're ready to go all out, you might want to invest in an air fryer lid. This will allow you to brown and crisp food right in the pot, so you can skip transferring recipes like ribs to the broiler.

THE FIVE MOST COMMON INSTANT POT MISTAKES AND HOW TO AVOID THEM

Once you get the hang of it, using an Instant Pot will be second nature. But there are several common mistakes that even seasoned pressure cooker enthusiasts can make.

Keeping these five mistakes in mind will help set you up for success. They can also prevent you from thinking your Instant Pot is broken when you really just need a new sealing ring, a costly mistake that I'll never make again.

1. **Not adding enough liquid.** Instant Pots work because steam builds up inside them, creating a high-pressure environment. If you don't add enough water or broth, there won't be enough steam produced, and the pot won't pressurize. A good rule of thumb is to add at least 1 cup of liquid to 6-quart models.

2. **Using too much liquid.** The sealed nature of pressure cookers means that, unlike stovetop cooking, liquid won't evaporate during the cooking process. Adding too much liquid can result in dishes coming out soggy and bland. Keep in mind that many ingredients, such as vegetables and meat, release additional liquid as they cook. Others, like rice and grains, absorb liquid. If your recipe comes out soggy, hit the Sauté button and simmer it uncovered for a few minutes to help the liquid reduce.

3. **Using a damaged sealing ring.** If your sealing ring is cracked or otherwise, damaged your pot will not come to pressure. Always be sure to check the sealing ring before starting to cook.

4. **Not adding ingredients in the correct order.** If the recipe instructs you to add things in a certain order, it's for a reason. Some ingredients, like dairy and tomato sauce, have a tendency to stick to the bottom of the pot and trigger a burn warning. It's important to layer ingredients in the right order—and don't stir unless the recipe tells you to!

5. **Not planning enough time.** Yes, the Instant Pot can dramatically reduce traditional cooking times. But it will take time for the pot to come to pressure as well as for that pressure to release. The recipes in this book all indicate how much time you should allow for each step, so be sure to read through each recipe carefully and plan ahead.

ABOUT THE RECIPES

In addition to prep time and cook time, each recipe also indicates the amount of time it will take the Instant Pot to come to pressure and how long it will take for that pressure to release. This will give you a more complete picture of how long you should anticipate the recipe to take from start to finish.

The recipes in this book were all designed to ensure your success and help you become comfortable with your Instant Pot, but note that they were developed in a standard 6-quart Instant Pot. If you're working with a different size or if you want to scale the recipes up or down, refer to the Models and Sizes section (page 2).

A few additional labels have been included to help you identify the easiest recipes:

30 Minutes or Less: These recipes are ready in under a half hour, including pressure build and pressure release times. If you're hungry, these recipes are for you!

5 Ingredients or Fewer: With the exception of salt, pepper, water, and oil, these recipes are all made with no more than five ingredients.

No Dirty Dishes: These recipes are made entirely in the Instant Pot without the use of any additional pots, bowls, or accessories.

STEEL-CUT OATMEAL
PAGE 23

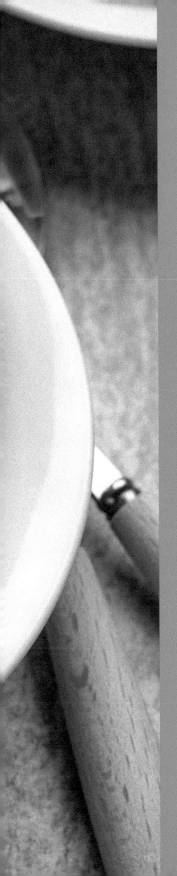

HAM-AND-CHEESE OMELET

SERVES: 4

PREP TIME: 10 minutes / **PRESSURE BUILD:** 5 minutes / **PRESSURE COOK:** 6 minutes / **QUICK RELEASE** / **TOTAL TIME:** 21 minutes

30 MINUTES OR LESS

Cooking this omelet in a Bundt pan set inside your pressure cooker results in a sliceable breakfast that's perfect for sharing.

Nonstick cooking spray	1 cup roughly chopped fresh baby spinach
5 large eggs	¼ cup chopped fresh flat-leaf parsley
2 tablespoons whole milk	¼ teaspoon garlic powder
½ cup chopped deli ham	¼ teaspoon red pepper flakes (optional)
½ cup shredded cheddar cheese	Salt
¼ cup sliced or cubed red bell pepper	Freshly ground black pepper

1. Grease a 7-inch Bundt pan with cooking spray.

2. In a medium bowl, whisk together the eggs and milk. Add all the remaining ingredients, season with salt and pepper, and stir to combine. Pour the mixture into the prepared pan. Do not cover the pan.

3. Set the trivet in the inner pot and pour in 1 cup of water. Place the Bundt pan on the trivet and lock the lid on the pressure cooker. Set the pressure valve to seal and cook for 6 minutes on manual high pressure. When the time is up, perform a quick release of pressure.

VARIATION TIP: Customize this omelet by adding precooked sausage, bacon, or ground chicken.

BISCUIT DUMPLINGS AND GRAVY

SERVES: 4

PREP TIME: 5 minutes / **SAUTÉ TIME:** 15 minutes / **PRESSURE BUILD:** 8 minutes / **PRESSURE COOK:** 5 minutes / **NATURAL RELEASE:** 5 minutes / **TOTAL TIME:** 38 minutes

Biscuits and gravy is a hearty breakfast that's full of flavor. Be sure to scrape the bottom of the pot well and let it cool for a few minutes before bringing it to pressure to help avoid a burn warning. If you have a nonstick insert, now is the time to use it.

1 tablespoon unsalted butter

1 pound pork sausage

¼ cup all-purpose flour

2⅓ cups whole milk, divided

2 teaspoons dried thyme

1 teaspoon salt

1½ teaspoons freshly ground black pepper, divided

¾ cup Bisquick or other baking mix

1. Melt the butter using the Sauté function of the pressure cooker. When melted, add the sausage and cook until browned, about 8 minutes. Break up the sausage as it cooks, leaving some bigger pieces for better texture.

2. Do not drain the pot. Add the flour and stir well. Continue to cook the flour and sausage mixture until brown, 2 to 3 minutes. Make sure to stir often.

3. When the mixture starts to brown, slowly add 2 cups of milk and mix; then add the thyme, salt, and ½ teaspoon of pepper. Scrape the bottom of the pot well to release any browned bits.

4. Turn the pot off and allow it to cool for 3 to 4 minutes.

5. In a medium bowl, mix together the Bisquick, remaining ⅓ cup of milk, and remaining 1 teaspoon of pepper. Stir until the dough just comes together.

6. Drop dollops of the dough into the sausage gravy and lock the lid on the pressure cooker. Set the pressure valve to seal and cook for 5 minutes on manual high pressure. Allow for a 5-minute natural release of pressure; then quick release any remaining pressure.

BANANA PANCAKE BITES

SERVES: 3

PREP TIME: 10 minutes / **PRESSURE BUILD:** 5 minutes / **PRESSURE COOK:** 7 minutes /
NATURAL RELEASE: 7 minutes / **TOTAL TIME:** 29 minutes

30 MINUTES OR LESS

Diced banana gives these pancake bites tons of flavor and contributes to their light, fluffy texture. Be careful when removing the pancakes from the mold as they will be very hot! Let them cool for a few minutes, and then press firmly on the bottom of each cup to release them from the mold.

Nonstick cooking spray

¾ cup all-purpose flour

1½ teaspoons baking powder

2 teaspoons sugar

¼ teaspoon salt

½ cup whole milk

1 large egg

1 tablespoon maple syrup

½ banana, diced

1. Spray a 7-cup silicone egg bite mold with cooking spray.

2. In a medium bowl, whisk together the flour, baking powder, sugar, and salt. In a measuring cup, whisk together the milk, egg, and syrup. Gently mix the wet ingredients into the dry ingredients. Stir in the banana.

3. Divide the batter between the cups of the prepared egg mold, filling each cup about three-quarters full. Cover the mold with the lid or with foil.

4. Set the trivet in the inner pot and pour in 1 cup of water. Place the egg bite mold on the trivet and lock the lid on the pressure cooker. Set the pressure valve to seal and cook for 7 minutes on manual high pressure. When the time is up, let the pressure release naturally for 7 minutes. Quick release any remaining pressure.

5. Remove the lid and let the pancake bites cool for a minute or two before inverting them onto a plate.

VARIATION TIP: Try replacing the banana with a diced apple or ¼ cup of blueberries.

SOUS VIDE EGG BITES

SERVES: 3

PREP TIME: 5 minutes / **PRESSURE BUILD:** 5 minutes / **PRESSURE COOK:** 12 minutes /
NATURAL RELEASE: 10 minutes / **TOTAL TIME:** 32 minutes

5 INGREDIENTS OR FEWER

These individually portioned egg bites are perfect for meal prep. I love making a batch of them and reheating in the microwave for super fast breakfasts all week long. If you don't have an egg bite mold, you can make these in 4-ounce canning jars. Be sure to look for jars that are labeled as being safe for pressure canning; other jars are not safe to use in a pressure cooker.

Nonstick cooking spray

4 large eggs

¼ cup cottage cheese

½ cup shredded cheddar cheese

4 cooked bacon slices, crumbled

1. Spray a 7-cup silicone egg bite mold with cooking spray.

2. In a medium bowl, whisk the eggs until they're fluffy. Beat in the cottage cheese until it is fully incorporated. (It's okay if there are still some lumps.) Stir in the cheddar cheese and bacon.

3. Divide the egg mixture among the cups of the prepared egg mold, filling each cup about three-quarters full. Cover the mold with the lid or with foil.

4. Set the trivet in the inner pot and pour in 1 cup of water. Place the egg bite mold on the trivet and lock the lid on the pressure cooker. Set the pressure valve to seal and cook for 12 minutes on manual high pressure. When the time is up, allow for a 10-minute natural release of the pressure; then quick release any remaining pressure.

5. Remove the lid and let the egg bites cool for a minute or two before inverting them onto a plate.

VARIATION TIP: Feel free to play with your mix-ins! You can swap ham, cooked sausage, or finely diced vegetables, like spinach or zucchini, for the bacon and use your favorite shredded cheese.

BOILED EGGS

SERVES: 6

PRESSURE BUILD: 5 minutes / **PRESSURE COOK:** 5 minutes (hard), 6 minutes (soft)/ **NATURAL RELEASE:** 5 minutes (hard), **QUICK RELEASE** (soft) / **TOTAL TIME:** 15 minutes (hard), 16 minutes (soft)

`30 MINUTES OR LESS`　　`5 INGREDIENTS OR FEWER`

Boiled eggs are always an Instant Pot fan-favorite because they come out perfectly cooked every time. Plus, they're super easy to peel. This recipe is written to make a half dozen eggs, but you can make as many as you want. Just be sure not to fill the pot past the Max Fill line.

6 large eggs

1. Set the trivet in the inner pot and pour in 1 cup of water.

2. Fill a large mixing bowl with ice water; set aside.

3. Stack the eggs on top of the trivet. Lock the lid on the pressure cooker. Set the pressure valve to seal.

4. **For hard-boiled eggs:** Cook for 5 minutes on manual high pressure. When the time is up, perform a natural release for 5 minutes; then quick release any remaining pressure. **For soft-boiled eggs**: Cook on manual low pressure for 6 minutes. When the time is up, perform a quick release of the pressure.

5. Carefully transfer the eggs to the ice water. Let them sit for 5 minutes to stop the cooking process; then peel.

> **COOKING TIP:** Use a steamer basket insert to make removing the eggs from the pot easier.

STEEL-CUT OATMEAL

SERVES: 4

PREP TIME: 5 minutes / **PRESSURE BUILD:** 13 minutes / **PRESSURE COOK:** 2 minutes / **NATURAL RELEASE:** 20 minutes / **TOTAL TIME:** 40 minutes

5 INGREDIENTS OR FEWER   **NO DIRTY DISHES**

Steel-cut oats have a nutty flavor and a chewy texture that makes them a delicious alternative to instant oatmeal or rolled oats, but they can take a long time to cook on the stove top. Thankfully, making them in a pressure cooker means they're ready in just over a half hour. They also reheat really well in the microwave, so go ahead and make a big batch so that you can enjoy a hearty breakfast all week long.

1 cup steel-cut oats

3 cups water

2 teaspoons vanilla extract

½ teaspoon ground cinnamon

½ teaspoon salt

2 tablespoons maple syrup

1. Combine the oats, water, vanilla, cinnamon, and salt in the pressure cooker and lock the lid on the cooker.

2. Cook for 2 minutes on manual high pressure. When the time is up, allow for full natural release of pressure, 15 to 20 minutes.

3. Stir in the maple syrup and serve with any other toppings you like.

VARIATION TIP: Add 2 chopped apples to the uncooked mixture and top each serving with a spoonful of peanut butter.

CINNAMON-SUGAR MONKEY BREAD

SERVES: 4

PREP TIME: 15 minutes / **PRESSURE BUILD:** 5 minutes / **PRESSURE COOK:** 10 minutes /
NATURAL RELEASE: 15 minutes / **TOTAL TIME:** 45 minutes

A lot of people assume pressure cookers are only good for making soups and stews, so you might be surprised to learn they're also great for making baked goods like this monkey bread. Instant Pot monkey bread is a soft and sticky treat that's oh-so-fun to rip apart. Add chopped pecans or walnuts for a nice crunch.

Nonstick cooking spray

¼ cup (½ stick) salted butter, plus
 2 tablespoons, melted, divided

½ cup packed light brown sugar

⅓ cup granulated sugar

2 tablespoons ground cinnamon

3 (7.5-ounce) cans refrigerated biscuits,
 quartered

1. Grease a 7-inch Bundt pan with cooking spray.

2. In a small bowl, combine ¼ cup of melted butter and the brown sugar. Pour the mixture into the bottom of the prepared pan.

3. In a separate small bowl, combine the granulated sugar and cinnamon. Roll each biscuit piece in the cinnamon-sugar mixture until evenly coated; then place them in the pan.

4. Once all the biscuit pieces are stacked evenly, pour the remaining 2 tablespoons of melted butter over the top. Cover with aluminum foil.

5. Set the trivet in the inner pot and pour in 1 cup of water. Place the covered pan on the trivet and lock the lid on the pressure cooker.

6. Set the pressure valve to seal and cook for 10 minutes on manual high pressure. When the time is up, allow for a 15-minute natural release of pressure; then quick release any remaining pressure.

7. Remove the foil from the pan and place a rimmed serving plate on top of the monkey bread. Flip it over in a swift motion to release the bread and enjoy at once.

VARIATION TIP: Add chopped pecans or walnuts for a nice crunch.

CHEESY GRITS

SERVES: 4

PREP TIME: 5 minutes / **SAUTÉ TIME:** 2 minutes / **PRESSURE BUILD:** 7 minutes / **PRESSURE COOK:** 10 minutes / **NATURAL RELEASE:** 15 minutes / **TOTAL TIME:** 39 minutes

5 INGREDIENTS OR FEWER   **NO DIRTY DISHES**

Making grits in an Instant Pot helps them come out perfectly smooth and lump-free every time. It also saves you from having to stand over the stove stirring the pot! Sautéing the grits in butter first keeps them from sticking to the pot, so be sure not to skip this important step.

2 tablespoons unsalted butter

1 cup stone-ground white grits

3 cups water

Salt

Freshly ground black pepper

¾ cup whole milk

½ cup shredded sharp or mild cheddar cheese (or more to taste)

1. Melt the butter using the Sauté function of the pressure cooker. When the butter is melted, add the grits and cook, stirring occasionally, for 2 minutes until fragrant.

2. Add the water and season with salt and pepper. Lock the lid on the pressure cooker. Set the pressure valve to seal and cook for 10 minutes on manual high pressure. When the time is up, allow for a 15-minute natural release of pressure; then quick release any remaining pressure.

3. Stir the milk into the grits, followed by the cheese. You can serve as is or cover and cook for 2 additional minutes for a creamier consistency. Season to taste and serve hot.

GO BIG: You can swap out the butter for bacon grease for a true Southern flavor.

SAUSAGE-AND-POTATO HASH

SERVES: 6

PREP TIME: 10 minutes / **SAUTÉ TIME:** 10 minutes / **PRESSURE BUILD:** 5 minutes / **PRESSURE COOK:** 2 minutes / **QUICK RELEASE** / **TOTAL TIME:** 27 minutes

30 MINUTES OR LESS

Thanks to the pressure cooker, this comfort food staple can be made entirely in one pot! Steaming the potatoes under pressure means this breakfast hash cooks up much quicker than stovetop versions. Using the Sauté function at the end crisps it up!

1½ pounds russet potatoes, peeled and cubed

2 tablespoons unsalted butter

½ pound ground sausage

½ teaspoon garlic powder

1 teaspoon onion powder

½ teaspoon paprika

½ teaspoon salt

½ teaspoon freshly ground black pepper

½ teaspoon dried thyme

1. Pour 1 cup of water into the inner pot. Place the potatoes in a steamer basket and lower the basket into the pot.

2. Lock the lid on the pressure cooker. Set the pressure valve to seal and cook for 2 minutes on manual high pressure. When the time is up, perform a quick release of pressure.

3. Remove the steamer basket and drain the liquid from the inner pot. Return the inner pot to the pressure cooker and turn on the Sauté function.

4. When it is hot, melt the butter. Add the sausage and cook until browned, 5 to 7 minutes.

5. Return the potatoes to the pot and stir in the remaining ingredients. Cook until browned, 2 to 3 minutes.

SPINACH-ARTICHOKE DIP
PAGE 30

Appetizers

SPINACH-ARTICHOKE DIP

SERVES: 6

PREP TIME: 10 minutes / **SAUTÉ TIME:** 5 minutes / **PRESSURE BUILD:** 5 minutes / **PRESSURE COOK:** 7 minutes / **NATURAL RELEASE:** 10 minutes / **TOTAL TIME:** 37 minutes

Spinach and artichoke dip is a classic for a reason: It's creamy, rich, and loaded with flavor. Using the pot-in-pot cooking method helps prevent this dairy-laden dip from burning. Serve this dip piping hot with plenty of bread cubes, tortilla chips, or pita wedges for dipping.

3 tablespoons unsalted butter

1 small onion, diced

3 garlic cloves, minced

8 ounces cream cheese, at room temperature

1 (14-ounce) can artichoke hearts, drained and chopped

1 (10-ounce) package frozen spinach, thawed, drained, and squeezed

½ cup shredded mozzarella cheese

½ cup finely grated Parmesan cheese

½ teaspoon Italian seasoning

1. Melt the butter using the Sauté function. Add the onion and garlic and cook until the onion starts to turn translucent, about 5 minutes.

2. In a medium bowl, mix together the cream cheese, artichokes, spinach, mozzarella, Parmesan, and Italian seasoning.

3. Add the cooked onions and garlic to the spinach mixture. Stir to combine.

4. Transfer the mixture to a 7-inch round cake pan.

5. Clean the inner pot and return it to the pressure cooker. Set the trivet in the inner pot and pour in 1 cup of water. Place the pan on the trivet.

6. Lock the lid on the pressure cooker. Set the pressure valve to seal and cook for 7 minutes on manual high pressure. When the time is up, allow for a 10-minute natural release of pressure; then quick release any remaining pressure.

7. Stir the dip to make sure everything is incorporated before serving.

COOKING TIP: For a delicious, crispy brown crust, sprinkle additional shredded mozzarella and Parmesan cheese on top and broil for about 5 minutes, or until golden brown.

CREAMY HUMMUS

SERVES: 4

PREP TIME: 5 minutes / **PRESSURE BUILD:** 13 minutes / **PRESSURE COOK:** 40 minutes / **NATURAL RELEASE:** 15 minutes / **TOTAL TIME:** 1 hour 13 minutes

NO DIRTY DISHES

Hummus made in a pressure cooker is incredibly smooth and creamy. Make it using dried chickpeas, also known as garbanzo beans. Unlike stovetop recipes, there's no need to soak the beans first.

1¼ cups dried chickpeas

6 cups water

2 whole garlic cloves, plus 10 cloves, minced

½ cup tahini paste

½ cup lemon juice

½ cup olive oil, divided

1¼ teaspoons kosher salt

1 teaspoon ground cumin

1. Combine the chickpeas, water, and whole garlic cloves in the inner pot. Lock the lid on the pressure cooker. Set the pressure valve to seal and cook for 40 minutes on manual high pressure. When the time is up, allow for a 15-minute natural release of pressure; then quick release any remaining pressure.

2. Remove the lid and reserve ½ cup of the cooking water; then drain the chickpeas and return them to the pot.

3. Add the tahini, minced garlic, lemon juice, ¼ cup of olive oil, and 1 tablespoon of reserved cooking liquid to the pot. Use an immersion blender to blend until smooth.

4. Add the salt, cumin, and remaining ¼ cup of olive oil. Mix well. Thin with additional cooking liquid, if desired.

MAKE AHEAD: This hummus is great in the refrigerator for up to 7 days and can be frozen for up to 4 months. If you plan on freezing your hummus, make it a little thicker by omitting the reserved cooking liquid in step 3. This will prevent it from getting too loose when it defrosts.

SWEET-AND-SOUR MEATBALLS

SERVES: 6

PREP TIME: 5 minutes / **SAUTÉ TIME:** 10 minutes / **PRESSURE BUILD:** 5 minutes / **PRESSURE COOK:** 5 minutes / **QUICK RELEASE** / **TOTAL TIME:** 25 minutes

30 MINUTES OR LESS

Sweet-and-sour meatballs are one of my favorite recipes! Thanks to the Instant Pot and store-bought frozen meatballs, it can be on the table in less than a half hour. Enjoy these meatballs as an appetizer, or turn them into a meal by serving them over rice.

2¼ cups pineapple juice, divided

½ cup packed light brown sugar

½ cup rice vinegar

1 tablespoon sriracha

¼ cup ketchup

1 tablespoon soy sauce

1 (24-ounce) bag frozen meatballs

1 tablespoon cornstarch

1 cup drained pineapple chunks

1. Turn on the Sauté function and, in the inner pot, combine 2 cups of pineapple juice with the brown sugar, vinegar, sriracha, ketchup, and soy sauce. Stir and bring to a boil.

2. Turn off the pressure cooker and add the frozen meatballs.

3. Lock the lid on the pressure cooker. Set the pressure valve to seal and cook for 5 minutes on manual high pressure. When the time is up, perform a quick release of pressure.

4. In a small bowl, whisk together the remaining ¼ cup of pineapple juice and the cornstarch until smooth to make a slurry.

5. Turn the Sauté function back on, and add the pineapple chunks and cornstarch slurry. Mix well and cook until the sauce thickens, about 5 minutes.

BARBECUE LITTLE SMOKIES WITH BACON

SERVES: 6

PREP TIME: 5 minutes / **SAUTÉ TIME:** 5 minutes / **PRESSURE BUILD:** 15 minutes / **PRESSURE COOK:** 3 minutes / **QUICK RELEASE** / **TOTAL TIME:** 28 minutes

`30 MINUTES OR LESS`   `5 INGREDIENTS OR FEWER`   `NO DIRTY DISHES`

This recipe is always a hit at parties and tailgates. For a festive twist, use canned cranberry sauce instead of the grape jelly.

½ pound thick-cut bacon, chopped

½ cup water

1 (28-ounce) bottle barbecue sauce

1 (16-ounce) jar grape jelly

2 (14-ounce) packages little smokies

1. Turn on the Sauté function, and when the inner pot is hot, cook the bacon until crispy, about 5 minutes.

2. Add the water and deglaze the pot, stirring to scrape up the browned bits from the bottom. Add the barbecue sauce and jelly. Stir to combine and then add the little smokies. Make sure the little smokies are covered with sauce.

3. Lock the lid on the pressure cooker and set the pressure valve to seal. Cook for 3 minutes on manual high pressure. When the time is up, perform a quick release of pressure. Give everything a quick stir before serving.

VARIATION TIP: If you like your little smokies spicier, add a tablespoon or two of chile sauce.

STEAMED CRAB LEGS WITH DIPPING SAUCE

SERVES: 4

PREP TIME: 5 minutes / **PRESSURE BUILD:** 5 minutes/ **PRESSURE COOK:** 4 minutes / **QUICK RELEASE** / **TOTAL TIME:** 14 minutes

`30 MINUTES OR LESS`

Crab legs might seem fancy, but thanks to the pressure cooker, they couldn't be easier! Cooking the crab legs under pressure helps infuse them with seasoning. A garlicky dipping sauce cooks right alongside the crab.

2 pounds snow crab legs (4 clusters)	¼ teaspoon salt
1 teaspoon Old Bay seasoning	¼ teaspoon freshly ground black pepper
4 tablespoons (½ stick) unsalted butter	½ tablespoon lemon juice
2 garlic cloves, minced	1 teaspoon chopped fresh flat-leaf parsley

1. Set the trivet in the inner pot and pour in 1 cup of water. Place the crab legs on the trivet, folding them at the joint to fit. Sprinkle evenly with the Old Bay seasoning.

2. In a small ramekin, combine the butter, garlic, salt, pepper, lemon juice, and parsley. Cover tightly with aluminum foil and place in the center of the crab legs.

3. Lock the lid on the pressure cooker. Set the pressure valve to seal and cook for 4 minutes on manual high pressure. When the time is up, perform a quick release of pressure.

4. Uncover the dipping sauce and mix well. Serve the legs and sauce immediately.

COOKING TIP: If you are cooking for a crowd, as soon as the pressure cooking is done, you can repeat the process using the same water. Since the pot and liquid are already warm, it will only take 1 to 2 minutes for it to come to pressure.

LOADED BUFFALO POTATO SKINS

SERVES: 4

PREP TIME: 10 minutes / **SAUTÉ TIME:** 3 minutes / **PRESSURE BUILD:** 5 minutes / **PRESSURE COOK:** 7 minutes / **QUICK RELEASE** / **TOTAL TIME:** 25 minutes

30 MINUTES OR LESS   5 INGREDIENTS OR FEWER

Loaded Buffalo potato skins are a hearty snack that's such fun to eat! Potato skins take a long time to make in the oven, but with the Instant Pot they're ready in under a half hour. Cooking the potatoes under pressure also makes the insides super light and fluffy, so they're so much easier to scoop out.

4 small red potatoes

¼ cup blue cheese or ranch salad
  dressing

2 tablespoons Buffalo wing sauce

¼ cup shredded cheddar cheese

2 scallions, chopped

1. Set the trivet in the inner pot and pour in 1 cup of water. Place the potatoes on the trivet and lock the lid on the pressure cooker. Set the pressure valve to seal and cook for 7 minutes on manual high pressure. When the time is up, perform a quick release of pressure.

2. Let the potatoes cool; then cut them in half and scoop out the flesh, leaving a ½-inch rim around the edge on the potato. Discard the inner potato or save it for another use. Brush the inside of each potato half with salad dressing and wing sauce. Divide the cheese evenly among the potato skins.

3. Remove the trivet from the Instant Pot and wipe the inner pot dry. Return the potatoes to the pot, cut-sides up. Press the Sauté button and replace the lid. Cook for 2 to 3 minutes, until the cheese is melted. Sprinkle with the scallions.

SPINACH-STUFFED MUSHROOMS

SERVES: 6

PREP TIME: 10 minutes / **SAUTÉ TIME:** 3 minutes / **PRESSURE BUILD:** 5 minutes / **PRESSURE COOK:** 5 minutes / **QUICK RELEASE** / **TOTAL TIME:** 23 minutes

30 MINUTES OR LESS

These savory stuffed mushrooms are a hit at holidays. Be sure not to over-crowd your pot, or they can release too much moisture and come out soggy. The mushrooms should all fit in a single layer on the trivet. If you want to make a double batch, you can cook the filling all at the same time. That way you can have a second set of mushrooms stuffed and ready to cook when the first ones come out of the pot.

12 white mushrooms

1 tablespoon unsalted butter

2 cups baby spinach, chopped

1 tablespoon minced shallot

⅓ cup grated Pecorino Romano cheese

1 teaspoon lemon juice

1. Remove the stems from the mushroom caps. Finely chop the stems.

2. Melt the butter using the Sauté function of the pressure cooker. When the butter has melted, add the spinach and shallot and cook until the spinach is wilted, 2 to 3 minutes. Stir in the mushroom stems, cheese, and lemon juice.

3. Divide the spinach mixture evenly among the mushroom caps.

4. Set the trivet in the inner pot and pour in 1 cup of water. Place the mush-rooms, filling-side up, on the trivet and lock the lid on the pressure cooker. Set the pressure valve to seal and cook for 5 minutes on manual high pres-sure. Quick release the pressure.

VARIATION TIP: For more texture, sprinkle the cooked mushrooms with toasted panko bread crumbs before serving.

MINESTRONE SOUP
PAGE 42

Soups, Stews, and Chili

LENTIL SOUP

SERVES: 4

PREP TIME: 10 minutes / **SAUTÉ TIME:** 6 minutes / **PRESSURE BUILD:** 10 minutes / **PRESSURE COOK:** 5 minutes / **NATURAL RELEASE:** 10 minutes / **TOTAL TIME:** 41 minutes

NO DIRTY DISHES

Lentil soup is not only delicious but also packed with protein, fiber, and other healthy nutrients. Taking a few minutes to sauté the vegetables in butter before adding the lentils will give this soup a richer, more complex flavor.

½ tablespoon unsalted butter

1 medium onion, diced

2 medium carrots, peeled and diced

2 medium celery stalks, diced

4 garlic cloves, minced

2 large tomatoes, chopped

1¼ cups whole dried lentils

½ teaspoon paprika

1 teaspoon ground cumin

4½ cups vegetable broth

Salt

Freshly ground black pepper

1. Turn on the Sauté function, and when the inner pot is hot, melt the butter. Stir in the onion, carrot, and celery; then sauté until they start to soften, about 3 minutes. Add the garlic and cook until fragrant, about 1 minute.

2. Add the tomatoes, lentils, paprika, and cumin. Cook for 2 to 3 minutes; then add the broth. Mix well and season with salt and pepper.

3. Lock the lid on the pressure cooker. Set the pressure valve to seal and cook for 5 minutes on manual high pressure. When the time is up, allow for a 10-minute natural release of pressure; then quick release any remaining pressure.

VARIATION TIP: Split lentils can overcook in soups, so I make this with brown lentils. Any type of whole lentil works great.

15-BEAN SOUP

SERVES: 8

PREP TIME: 5 minutes / **PRESSURE BUILD:** 15 minutes / **PRESSURE COOK:** 40 minutes /
NATURAL RELEASE: 20 minutes / **TOTAL TIME:** 1 hour 20 minutes

NO DIRTY DISHES

This hearty bean soup will stick to your ribs and warm you up on even the coldest winter nights. For the tastiest results, throw away the sodium-laden seasoning packet that's sold with the beans and use seasonings from your spice rack instead. This recipe is a great way to use up leftover ham from the holidays, but if you don't have any, a diced ham steak also works well.

1 (20-ounce) package 15-bean soup mix (such as Hurst HamBeens), spice packet discarded, beans rinsed

1 medium onion, diced

2 garlic cloves, minced

2 bay leaves

1½ teaspoons dried thyme

7 cups chicken broth

1 teaspoon hot sauce

1 pound diced ham

Salt

Freshly ground black pepper

1. Combine the beans, onion, garlic, bay leaves, thyme, broth, hot sauce, and ham in the inner pot and lock the lid on the pressure cooker.

2. Set the pressure valve to seal and cook for 40 minutes on manual high pressure.

3. When the time is up, allow for a 20-minute natural release of pressure; then quick release any remaining pressure.

4. Discard the bay leaves and season with salt and pepper to taste.

COOKING TIP: The longer you let your soup sit, the thicker it will get. If you are reheating leftovers, add a splash of water or broth to thin the soup to your desired consistency.

MINESTRONE SOUP

SERVES: 6

PREP TIME: 10 minutes / **SAUTÉ TIME:** 13 minutes / **PRESSURE BUILD:** 15 minutes / **PRESSURE COOK:** 15 minutes / **QUICK RELEASE** / **TOTAL TIME:** 53 minutes

NO DIRTY DISHES

Minestrone is a hearty Italian soup made with vegetables, beans, and pasta. Cooking the pasta under pressure can release its starch and thicken the broth too much, so add it at the very end and use the Sauté function to simmer it until it's done.

½ cup olive oil

5 large garlic cloves, minced

1 medium onion, diced

3 medium carrots, peeled and diced

2 celery stalks, diced

2 (14.5-ounce) cans diced tomatoes

2 medium russet potatoes, cut into
   ¼-inch chunks

1 zucchini, unpeeled, diced

2 (15-ounce) cans cannellini beans,
   drained and rinsed

1 (15-ounce) can dark red kidney beans,
   drained and rinsed

4 cups chicken broth

1 cup water

1 teaspoon Italian seasoning

1 tablespoon chopped fresh
   flat-leaf parsley

Salt

Freshly ground black pepper

1 cup ditalini or other small pasta

1. Turn on the Sauté function, and when the inner pot is hot, pour in the oil. Stir in the garlic, onion, carrot, and celery and sauté until soft, about 5 minutes.

2. Add the tomatoes and their juices, potatoes, zucchini, beans, chicken broth, and water. Add the Italian seasoning and parsley, season with salt and pepper, and stir well.

3. Lock the lid on the pressure cooker. Set the pressure valve to seal and cook for 15 minutes on manual high pressure. When the time is up, perform a quick release of pressure.

4. Take off the lid, turn the Sauté function back on, and add the pasta. Cook until al dente, about 8 minutes.

CHICKEN NOODLE SOUP

SERVES: 6

PREP TIME: 5 minutes / **SAUTÉ TIME:** 11 minutes / **PRESSURE BUILD:** 18 minutes / **PRESSURE COOK:** 20 minutes / **NATURAL RELEASE:** 10 minutes / **TOTAL TIME:** 1 hour 4 minutes

`NO DIRTY DISHES`

Making chicken noodle soup in a pressure cooker means you can have that simmered-all-day flavor in just about an hour! Stirring flat-leaf parsley into the finished soup gives it an extra pop of fresh flavor.

1 tablespoon olive oil

1 small onion, diced

4 garlic cloves, minced

5 carrots, peeled and cut into
  ½-inch pieces

2 celery stalks, cut into ½-inch pieces

1 (3- to 4-pound) chicken, giblets removed
  and discarded

2 tablespoons soy sauce

8 cups water

2 teaspoons salt

1 teaspoon freshly ground black pepper

4 ounces extra wide egg noodles

¼ cup minced fresh flat-leaf parsley,
  for garnish

1. Turn on the Sauté function, and when the inner pot is hot, pour in the oil. Stir in the onion and cook until it starts to soften, 3 to 4 minutes.

2. Add the garlic, carrot, and celery and sauté for 1 to 2 minutes. Place the chicken in the pot. Add the soy sauce, water, salt, and pepper.

3. Lock the lid on the pressure cooker. Set the pressure valve to seal and cook for 20 minutes on manual high pressure. When the time is up, allow for a 10-minute natural release of pressure; then quick release any remaining pressure.

4. Remove the chicken from the pot. When it's cool enough to handle, shred the meat and discard the bones.

5. Turn the Sauté function back on and add the egg noodles. Cook for 5 minutes, or until soft; then return the shredded chicken to the pot.

6. Add the parsley, adjust the seasonings to taste, and serve.

CHICKEN POTPIE SOUP

SERVES: 6

PREP TIME: 10 minutes / **SAUTÉ TIME:** 10 minutes / **PRESSURE BUILD:** 9 minutes / **PRESSURE COOK:** 3 minutes / **NATURAL RELEASE:** 10 minutes / **TOTAL TIME:** 42 minutes

NO DIRTY DISHES

This warming soup tastes exactly like the creamy filling in my favorite chicken potpie. For the most authentic flavor, serve this soup over freshly baked biscuits.

2 tablespoons olive oil

3 pounds boneless, skinless chicken breasts, cut into 1- to 1½-inch bite-size pieces

1 small onion, chopped

3 medium celery stalks, cut into ½-inch pieces

4 garlic cloves, minced

3 medium russet potatoes, peeled and cut into 1-inch cubes

12 ounces frozen mixed vegetables (peas, carrots, corn, and green beans)

3½ cups low-sodium chicken broth

2 teaspoons dried sage

1 teaspoon dried thyme

2 teaspoons Italian seasoning

2 teaspoons freshly ground black pepper

3 ounces cream cheese, cubed

½ cup freshly grated Parmesan cheese

1 cup heavy (whipping) cream

1. Turn on the Sauté function, and when the inner pot is hot, pour in the oil. Stir in the chicken, onion, and celery and cook until the chicken turns white on the outside, 3 to 5 minutes. Add the garlic and cook until fragrant, about 1 minute. Then add the potatoes, frozen veggies, broth, sage, thyme, Italian seasoning, and pepper.

2. Lock the lid on the pressure cooker. Set the pressure valve to seal and cook for 3 minutes on manual high pressure. When the time is up, allow for a 10-minute natural release of pressure; then quick release any remaining pressure.

3. Turn the Sauté function back on and add the cream cheese, Parmesan, and cream. Stir well. Turn the pressure cooker off and let the soup sit for 5 minutes to thicken.

LASAGNA SOUP

SERVES: 6

PREP TIME: 10 minutes / **SAUTÉ TIME:** 7 minutes / **PRESSURE BUILD:** 14 minutes / **PRESSURE COOK:** 5 minutes / **QUICK RELEASE** / **TOTAL TIME:** 36 minutes

`NO DIRTY DISHES`

This weeknight take on lasagna has all the flavor of our favorite meal in a warm and hearty soup. If you don't like sausage, feel free to swap it out for ground chicken, turkey, or beef. You can use broken up regular lasagna noodles if you can't find mini ones, but the soup will come out thinner.

1 pound mild ground Italian sausage

½ teaspoon salt

¼ teaspoon freshly ground black pepper

½ teaspoon Italian seasoning

1 small onion, diced

3 garlic cloves, minced

3 cups water, divided

4 cups dry mini lasagna noodles

1 (25-ounce) jar marinara sauce

1 cup ricotta cheese

1 cup shredded mozzarella cheese

1. Turn on the Sauté function, and when the inner pot is hot, put in the sausage, salt, pepper, and Italian seasoning. Cook, stirring to break up the sausage, until it starts to brown lightly; then add the onion and garlic. Cook until the meat is thoroughly browned, 5 to 7 minutes.

2. Add 1 cup of water and deglaze the pot, stirring to scrape up the browned bits from the bottom.

3. Add the noodles, marinara sauce, and remaining 2 cups of water. Use the back of a spoon to gently push down any noodles that are not submerged, but do not stir.

4. Lock the lid on the pressure cooker. Set the pressure valve to seal and cook for 5 minutes on manual high pressure. When the time is up, perform a quick release of pressure.

5. Remove the lid and stir in the ricotta. Add the mozzarella and replace the lid. Allow the pot to sit undisturbed for 5 minutes to melt the cheese and then serve.

BEEF STEW

SERVES: 8

PREP TIME: 10 minutes / **SAUTÉ TIME:** 18 minutes / **PRESSURE BUILD:** 8 minutes / **PRESSURE COOK:** 30 minutes / **NATURAL RELEASE:** 10 minutes / **TOTAL TIME:** 1 hour 16 minutes

`NO DIRTY DISHES`

Electric pressure cookers are perfect for making rich stews like this one. Using the Sauté function to brown the beef gives this stew its classic flavor. Be sure not to crowd the pot during this step—add the beef in batches if necessary or it can steam instead of browning.

3 tablespoons olive oil

2½ pounds beef chuck roast, cut into 1½-inch pieces

1 large onion, diced

1½ cups chopped celery

2 tablespoons minced garlic

¼ cup balsamic vinegar

3 cups beef broth

3 tablespoons tomato paste

4 cups halved baby potatoes

1½ cups peeled and chopped carrots

2 teaspoons salt

2 teaspoons freshly ground black pepper

1 teaspoon dried thyme

1 teaspoon dried rosemary

1 teaspoon dried oregano

1. Turn on the Sauté function, and when the inner pot is hot, pour in the oil. Add the meat, working in batches if necessary, and brown it 2 to 3 minutes on each side. Don't try to cook it; you are just searing it at this point.

2. Add the onion and celery and cook until the onion is translucent, 3 to 4 minutes. Add the garlic and cook until fragrant, about 1 minute.

3. Pour in the balsamic vinegar and deglaze the pot, stirring to scrape up the browned bits from the bottom.

4. Add the remaining ingredients. Lock the lid on the pressure cooker. Set the pressure valve to seal and cook for 30 minutes on manual high pressure. When the time is up, allow for a 10-minute natural release of pressure; then quick release any remaining pressure.

5. Scoop into bowls and serve.

RANCH WHITE CHICKEN CHILI

SERVES: 8

PREP TIME: 10 minutes / **PRESSURE BUILD:** 7 minutes / **PRESSURE COOK:** 20 minutes / **NATURAL RELEASE:** 10 minutes / **TOTAL TIME:** 47 minutes

Ranch seasoning gives this chicken chili a zesty kick while cream cheese contributes to its velvety texture. I like to use a combination of black and white beans in this recipe, but you can substitute whatever canned beans you have in your pantry.

2 large boneless, skinless chicken breasts

1 (15-ounce) can black beans, drained and rinsed

1 (15-ounce) can white beans, drained and rinsed

1 medium onion, chopped

2 cups frozen corn

1 (10-ounce) can diced tomatoes and green chiles

1 cup chicken broth

1 teaspoon chili powder

1 teaspoon ground cumin

1 (0.4-ounce) packet ranch dressing mix

8 ounces cream cheese, cut into 6 pieces

1. Combine the chicken, black beans, white beans, onion, corn, tomatoes, and chicken broth in the inner pot. Sprinkle with the chili powder, cumin, and ranch dressing mix and stir well.

2. Lock the lid on the pressure cooker. Set the pressure valve to seal and cook for 20 minutes on manual high pressure. When the time is up, allow for a 10-minute natural release of pressure; then quick release any remaining pressure.

3. Transfer the chicken to a plate and shred it with a fork. Add the cream cheese to the bean mixture and stir until the cheese is melted and combined.

4. Return the chicken to the pot and stir well.

SHRIMP PAELLA
PAGE 59

CREAMY POLENTA

SERVES: 4

PREP TIME: 5 minutes / **PRESSURE BUILD:** 9 minutes / **PRESSURE COOK:** 9 minutes /
NATURAL RELEASE: 15 minutes / **TOTAL TIME:** 38 minutes

`5 INGREDIENTS OR FEWER`   `NO DIRTY DISHES`

*If you've ever tried making polenta on the stove, you know how it likes to spit
and sputter. I've been burned more times than I can count! This version elim-
inates that risk, since you can keep the cover on. It comes out just as creamy
and flavorful as more traditional methods. For this recipe, look for dry cornmeal sold in a box or bag, not prepared polenta sold in a log.*

1 cup dry cornmeal

4 cups water

1 teaspoon salt

1 teaspoon freshly ground black pepper

3 tablespoons unsalted butter

½ cup freshly grated Parmesan cheese

1. Combine the cornmeal, water, salt, and pepper in the inner pot and stir well.

2. Lock the lid on the pressure cooker. Set the pressure valve to seal and cook
   for 9 minutes on manual high pressure. When the time is up, allow for a
   15-minute natural release of pressure.

3. Remove the lid and whisk in the butter and Parmesan. Keep stirring until
   everything is well combined. Generously season with additional salt and
   pepper to taste.

HAM-AND-GREENS BARLEY

SERVES: 4

PREP TIME: 5 minutes / **SAUTÉ TIME:** 7 minutes / **PRESSURE BUILD:** 11 minutes / **PRESSURE COOK:** 18 minutes / **QUICK RELEASE** / **TOTAL TIME:** 41 minutes

NO DIRTY DISHES

Barley makes a great base for this hearty dinner. Be sure to use hulled barley, which has the flavorful bran layer intact, as opposed to more processed pearl barley, since they don't cook at the same rate.

1 tablespoon unsalted butter

1 cup hulled barley

¼ cup finely chopped onion

4 cups water

½ teaspoon salt

½ cup diced cooked ham

½ cup mustard greens

4 eggs, cooked to your preference

1. Turn on the Sauté function, and when the inner pot is hot, melt the butter. Stir in the barley and onion and sauté until the barley starts to toast, 1 to 2 minutes. Add the water and salt and give everything a stir.

2. Lock the lid on the pressure cooker. Set the pressure valve to seal and cook for 18 minutes on manual high pressure. When the time is up, perform a quick release of pressure. If there is liquid remaining, you can drain it if you wish.

3. Turn the Sauté function back on and add the ham and greens. Cook until the greens are just wilted, about 5 minutes.

4. Scoop one-fourth of the barley into each bowl and top with an egg done however you like it.

COOKING TIP: You want the barley to be chewy but not crunchy. If you release pressure and it's not quite done, simply leave the remaining liquid in the pot and let it simmer a few minutes before adding the ham and greens.

ENCHILADA QUINOA

SERVES: 4

PREP TIME: 5 minutes / **PRESSURE BUILD:** 8 minutes / **PRESSURE COOK:** 1 minute /
NATURAL RELEASE: 15 minutes / **TOTAL TIME:** 29 minutes

`30 MINUTES OR LESS` `NO DIRTY DISHES`

You've heard of burrito bowls, but how about enchilada bowls? Quinoa is a quick-cooking seed that forms a delicious base for bowls like this one. Be sure to rinse the quinoa well before cooking it, or it can become bitter. Enjoy these bowls straight from the pot or top them with your favorite enchilada toppings, like avocado, cilantro, or sour cream.

½ small onion, diced

1 (4.3-ounce) can mild green chiles

1 (10-ounce) bag frozen corn

1 (15-ounce) can black beans, drained and rinsed

1 cup chopped fresh tomatoes

1 teaspoon chili powder

½ teaspoon ground cumin

¼ teaspoon salt

1 cup uncooked quinoa, rinsed well

2 cups water

1 cup enchilada sauce

1 cup shredded Monterey Jack cheese

1. Combine the onion, chiles, corn, beans, tomatoes, chili powder, cumin, salt, quinoa, and water in the inner pot and stir well.

2. Lock the lid on the pressure cooker. Set the pressure valve to seal and cook for 1 minute on manual high pressure. When the time is up, allow for a 15-minute natural release of pressure; then quick release any remaining pressure.

3. Stir in the enchilada sauce and cheese.

MAKE AHEAD: You can store this in the refrigerator for up to 4 days or portion it into meal-size amounts and freeze for up to 3 months. Thaw frozen portions in the refrigerator overnight, then reheat in the microwave.

PARMESAN RISOTTO

SERVES: 6

PREP TIME: 5 minutes / **SAUTÉ TIME:** 7 minutes / **PRESSURE BUILD:** 5 minutes / **PRESSURE COOK:** 5 minutes / **NATURAL RELEASE:** 5 minutes / **TOTAL TIME:** 27 minutes

`30 MINUTES OR LESS`   `NO DIRTY DISHES`

You'll love this Instant Pot risotto, which makes the days of standing over the stove endlessly stirring obsolete. Be sure to scrape up any browned bits in step 2 to avoid getting a burn warning.

5 tablespoons salted butter, divided	4 cups chicken broth
1 medium onion, diced	1 tablespoon dried thyme
3 garlic cloves, minced	1 teaspoon salt
2 cups Arborio rice	½ teaspoon freshly ground black pepper
½ cup white wine	½ cup freshly grated Parmesan cheese

1. Turn on the Sauté function, and when the inner pot is hot, melt 2 tablespoons of the butter. Add the onion and sauté until it starts to soften, about 3 minutes. Add the garlic and cook until fragrant, about 1 minute.

2. Add the rice and cook for 3 minutes, stirring frequently. Add the wine and deglaze the pot, stirring to scrape up the browned bits from the bottom. Make sure nothing is stuck.

3. Add the chicken broth, thyme, salt, and pepper. Stir to combine.

4. Lock the lid on the pressure cooker. Set the pressure valve to seal and cook for 5 minutes on manual high pressure. When the time is up, allow for a 5-minute natural release of pressure; then quick release any remaining pressure.

5. Add the remaining 3 tablespoons of butter and the Parmesan to the rice and stir well. Season with additional salt and pepper to taste.

COOKING TIP: When you take off the lid, the risotto will look liquidy. Don't worry! Once you stir everything, it will come together nicely and thicken up.

RICE PILAF

SERVES: 4

PREP TIME: 10 minutes / **SAUTÉ TIME:** 7 minutes / **PRESSURE BUILD:** 5 minutes / **PRESSURE COOK:** 3 minutes / **NATURAL RELEASE:** 15 minutes / **TOTAL TIME:** 40 minutes

`NO DIRTY DISHES`

Vermicelli, a thin pasta similar to angel hair, gives this rice pilaf its classic texture. Using the Sauté function to toast the vermicelli and rice before adding the liquid gives this dish an extra layer of flavor.

4 tablespoons (½ stick) unsalted butter

⅓ cup vermicelli, broken into
  ½-inch pieces

1 cup long-grain white rice

1½ cups chicken broth

1 teaspoon garlic powder

¾ teaspoon salt

¼ teaspoon freshly ground black pepper

½ teaspoon onion powder

¼ teaspoon paprika

1 teaspoon dried parsley

1. Turn on the Sauté function, and when the inner pot is hot, melt the butter. Stir in the vermicelli and cook until browned, 2 to 3 minutes; then add the rice. Cook until the rice starts to toast, another 3 to 4 minutes.

2. Add the chicken broth and the remaining ingredients to the rice mixture. Stir well, scraping up any browned bits from the bottom of the pot.

3. Lock the lid on the pressure cooker. Set the pressure valve to seal and cook for 3 minutes on manual high pressure. When the time is up, allow for a 15-minute natural release of pressure; then quick release any remaining pressure.

4. Open the lid and give everything a good stir.

COOKING TIP: If there is any liquid remaining in the pressure cooker, you can hit the Keep Warm button and let it sit for another 5 minutes until absorbed.

COCONUT RICE

SERVES: 6

PREP TIME: 5 minutes / **PRESSURE BUILD:** 7 minutes / **PRESSURE COOK:** 5 minutes / **NATURAL RELEASE:** 10 minutes / **TOTAL TIME:** 27 minutes

`30 MINUTES OR LESS`   `5 INGREDIENTS OR FEWER`   `NO DIRTY DISHES`

Cooking rice in coconut milk and broth results in a creamy dish that's packed with flavor. It's the perfect side dish to serve with spicy Thai- or Caribbean-inspired dishes.

1½ cups jasmine rice, rinsed
1 (14-ounce) can unsweetened coconut milk

½ cup chicken broth
¼ teaspoon salt

1. Combine the rice, coconut milk, broth, and salt in the inner pot. Lock the lid on the pressure cooker. Set the pressure valve to seal and cook for 5 minutes on manual high pressure. When the time is up, allow for a 10-minute natural release of pressure; then quick release any remaining pressure.

2. Fluff the rice with a fork and serve.

MAKE AHEAD: You can easily double this recipe and freeze it in individual portions for up to 3 months. Note that it will take about 9 minutes for the pot to come to pressure if you double the recipe.

MUSHROOM BROWN RICE

SERVES: 4

PREP TIME: 10 minutes / **SAUTÉ TIME:** 10 minutes / **PRESSURE BUILD:** 5 minutes / **PRESSURE COOK:** 25 minutes / **QUICK RELEASE** / **TOTAL TIME:** 50 minutes

NO DIRTY DISHES

I love the earthy flavor of baby bella (cremini) mushrooms in this recipe, but feel free to substitute your favorites. Serve this brown rice as a side dish or mix in some cooked chicken and veggies, like peas, to transform it into a full meal.

3 tablespoons unsalted butter, divided

1 small onion, diced

3 garlic cloves, minced

1 pound baby bella mushrooms, sliced

2 teaspoons Worcestershire sauce

½ teaspoon dried thyme

1 cup long-grain brown rice

1¼ cups vegetable broth

Salt

Freshly ground black pepper

1. Turn on the Sauté function, and when the inner pot is hot, melt 1 tablespoon of the butter. Stir in the onion and sauté until it starts to soften, about 3 minutes. Add the garlic and cook until fragrant, about 1 minute.

2. Add the mushrooms, Worcestershire sauce, and thyme. Cook, stirring occasionally, until the mushrooms reduce in size, 5 to 6 minutes.

3. When the mushroom mixture is ready, stir in the rice and broth. Lock the lid on the pressure cooker. Set the pressure valve to seal and cook for 25 minutes on manual high pressure. When the time is up, perform a quick release of pressure.

4. Add the remaining 2 tablespoons of butter and stir to combine. Season with salt and pepper.

INGREDIENT TIP: If some liquid remains after you release the pressure, don't worry; it will thicken if you let it stand for 2 or 3 minutes. The important thing is the texture of the rice; it should be slightly chewy but not crunchy.

SPANISH RICE

SERVES: 4

PREP TIME: 5 minutes / **SAUTÉ TIME:** 4 minutes / **PRESSURE BUILD:** 6 minutes / **PRESSURE COOK:** 5 minutes / **NATURAL RELEASE:** 10 minutes / **TOTAL TIME:** 30 minutes

30 MINUTES OR LESS   NO DIRTY DISHES

Made with simple ingredients, this flavorful rice goes with just about any-thing. It's fantastic with grilled chicken or shrimp, and leftovers are perfect for spur-of-the-moment burrito bowls.

1 tablespoon unsalted butter

1 small red bell pepper, seeded and chopped

1 small onion, chopped

3 garlic cloves, minced

1 cup long-grain white rice

2 tablespoons tomato paste

1 tablespoon ground cumin

1 teaspoon paprika

½ jalapeño pepper, seeded and diced

1½ cups water

Salt

Freshly ground black pepper

1. Turn on the Sauté function, and when the inner pot is hot, melt the butter. Stir in the bell pepper and onion and sauté until they start to soften, about 3 minutes. Add the garlic and cook until fragrant, about 1 minute.

2. Turn off the pressure cooker; then add the rice, tomato paste, cumin, paprika, jalapeño, and water. Stir to combine.

3. Lock the lid on the pressure cooker. Set the pressure valve to seal and cook for 5 minutes on manual high pressure. When the time is up, allow for a 10-minute natural release of pressure; then quick release any remaining pressure.

4. Fluff the rice with a fork, season with salt and pepper, and serve.

VARIATION TIP: If you want to make this recipe a little healthier, opt for brown rice instead of white. You will need to use 1 cup to 1 ¼ cup rice-to-water ratio, and you will also have to increase the cook time to 20 minutes.

HOPPING JOHN

SERVES: 6

PREP TIME: 10 minutes / **SAUTÉ TIME:** 5 minutes / **PRESSURE BUILD:** 7 minutes / **PRESSURE COOK:** 12 minutes / **NATURAL RELEASE:** 10 minutes / **TOTAL TIME:** 44 minutes

`NO DIRTY DISHES`

It's a tradition in the American South to eat black-eyed peas and rice on New Year's Day for good luck. Thanks to the pressure cooker, this delicious dish can be made in under an hour, so you can eat it any day of the year.

2 tablespoons olive oil

1 medium yellow onion, diced

1 medium carrot, peeled and diced

2 celery stalks, diced

1 small jalapeño, diced

3 garlic cloves, minced

1 tablespoon apple cider vinegar

6 thyme sprigs

1 bay leaf

1 cup long-grain white rice

2 teaspoons sea salt

2½ cups chicken or vegetable broth

28 ounces frozen black-eyed peas

1. Turn on the Sauté function and pour in the oil. When hot, stir in the onion, carrot, celery, and jalapeño. Cook for about 4 minutes, stirring frequently, until fragrant. Add the garlic, vinegar, thyme, and bay leaf and cook for 1 minute.

2. Add the rice, salt, chicken broth, and peas. Stir well.

3. Lock the lid on the pressure cooker. Set the pressure valve to seal and cook for 12 minutes on manual high pressure. When the time is up, allow for a 10-minute natural release of pressure; then quick release any remaining pressure.

4. Remove the thyme sprigs and bay leaf before serving.

COOKING TIP: If using dried beans, you will need to cook them for 8 minutes before adding the rice and then quick release the pressure. Add the rice and 2 additional cups of broth and cook as directed in step 3.

SHRIMP PAELLA

SERVES: 4

PREP TIME: 5 minutes / **SAUTÉ TIME:** 5 minutes / **PRESSURE BUILD:** 6 minutes / **PRESSURE COOK:** 5 minutes / **QUICK RELEASE** / **TOTAL TIME:** 21 minutes

`30 MINUTES OR LESS`   `NO DIRTY DISHES`

While paella cooked in a pressure cooker won't get the traditional crispy bottom of stovetop versions, it comes together in a fraction of the time with a deep, delicious flavor. Use frozen raw shrimp in their shells for this recipe; this will help prevent them from cooking too quickly and getting rubbery.

4 tablespoons (½ stick) unsalted butter

1 medium red bell pepper, seeded and diced

4 garlic cloves, minced

1½ cups chicken broth

1 cup jasmine rice, rinsed

¼ cup chopped fresh flat-leaf parsley

1 teaspoon salt

¼ teaspoon freshly ground black pepper

¼ teaspoon red pepper flakes

Juice of 1 medium lemon

¼ teaspoon saffron

1 pound frozen wild shrimp (16–20 count), shells and tails on

½ cup frozen peas, thawed

1. Turn on the Sauté function, and when the inner pot is hot, melt the butter. Stir in the bell pepper and garlic and cook until the peppers start to soften, about 4 minutes.

2. Add just enough broth to deglaze the pot, stirring to scrape up the browned bits from the bottom. Add the rice, parsley, salt, black pepper, red pepper flakes, lemon juice, saffron, and remaining chicken broth to the pot and place the shrimp on top. Do not stir.

3. Lock the lid on the pressure cooker. Set the pressure valve to seal and cook for 5 minutes on manual high pressure. When the time is up, perform a quick release of pressure.

4. Gently remove the cooked shrimp from the rice and peel them. Return the shrimp to the rice. Stir in the peas and serve.

CHICKEN FRIED RICE

SERVES: 4

PREP TIME: 5 minutes / **SAUTÉ TIME:** 3 minutes / **PRESSURE BUILD:** 5 minutes / **PRESSURE COOK:** 3 minutes / **NATURAL RELEASE:** 10 minutes / **TOTAL TIME:** 26 minutes

`30 MINUTES OR LESS`

Rinsing the rice prevents it from getting too sticky. Put the rice in a bowl of water and swirl it around until the water is cloudy; then drain in a fine-mesh strainer and rinse again. Repeat until the water runs clear. Be sure to scrape the crispy bits of rice up from the bottom of the pot before serving it for the most authentic fried rice flavor.

2 teaspoons vegetable oil, divided

2 eggs, whisked

3 garlic cloves, minced

1¼ cups chicken broth

1 pound boneless, skinless chicken breasts, cubed

1 cup peeled and diced carrots

1½ cups jasmine rice, rinsed

3 tablespoons soy sauce

½ teaspoon toasted sesame oil

½ cup frozen peas, thawed

Sesame seeds, for garnish (optional)

1. Turn on the Sauté function and pour in 1 teaspoon of the oil. When the oil is hot, add the eggs and push them around with a spatula to scramble them until they are fully cooked. Transfer the eggs to a plate and set aside. Bits of egg will be stuck to the bottom of the pot, but that's okay.

2. Pour in and heat the remaining 1 teaspoon of oil; then add the garlic. Sauté until fragrant, about 1 minute. Turn off the pressure cooker, add the chicken broth, and stir to scrape up all the browned bits from the bottom of the pot.

3. Add the chicken, carrot, and rice. Do not stir; just press the rice down to submerge it.

4. Lock the lid on the pressure cooker. Set the pressure valve to seal and cook for 3 minutes on manual high pressure. When the time is up, allow for a 10-minute natural release of pressure; then quick release any remaining pressure.

5. Stir in the soy sauce and sesame oil until the rice is well coated. Add the peas and scrambled eggs and stir to combine.

6. Place the lid back on the pressure cooker and let it sit undisturbed for 5 minutes to warm the peas and eggs. Toss with sesame seeds (if using) and serve immediately.

CHEESY CHICKEN, BROCCOLI, AND RICE CASSEROLE

SERVES: 4

PREP TIME: 5 minutes / **SAUTÉ TIME:** 6 minutes / **PRESSURE BUILD:** 5 minutes / **PRESSURE COOK:** 5 minutes / **NATURAL RELEASE:** 5 minutes / **TOTAL TIME:** 26 minutes

`30 MINUTES OR LESS`   `NO DIRTY DISHES`

This creamy casserole is a simple and delicious meal any night of the week. If you omit the chicken, it also makes a great holiday side dish—saving you precious space in the oven.

2 tablespoons unsalted butter

2 pounds boneless, skinless chicken breasts, cubed

1 small onion, diced

2 garlic cloves, minced

1⅓ cups chicken broth

1 teaspoon salt

¾ teaspoon freshly ground black pepper

1 teaspoon garlic powder

1⅓ cups long-grain rice

½ cup whole milk

2 cups shredded mild cheddar cheese

2 cups frozen broccoli florets, thawed

1. Turn on the Sauté function, and when the inner pot is hot, melt the butter. Add the chicken and onion and cook until the onion starts to turn translucent, about 5 minutes. Add the garlic and cook until fragrant, about 1 minute.

2. Add the broth, salt, pepper, and garlic powder. Stir to combine. Add the rice; do not stir, but press down to make sure it's submerged.

3. Lock the lid on the pressure cooker. Set the pressure valve to seal and cook for 5 minutes on manual high pressure. When the time is up, allow for a 5-minute natural release of pressure; then quick release any remaining pressure.

4. Stir in the milk and cheese; then add the broccoli and stir again. Cover the pot and let sit for 2 or 3 minutes to melt the cheese and heat the broccoli.

VARIATION TIP: For brown rice, increase the amount of broth to 1⅔ cup and cook for 15 minutes with a 10-minute natural release of pressure.

CHICKEN BURRITO BOWLS

SERVES: 5

PREP TIME: 5 minutes / **SAUTÉ TIME:** 5 minutes / **PRESSURE BUILD:** 7 minutes / **PRESSURE COOK:** 10 minutes / **NATURAL RELEASE:** 5 minutes / **TOTAL TIME:** 32 minutes

NO DIRTY DISHES

Burrito bowls were the first thing I made when I got my Instant Pot, and they're still one of my favorite recipes. Top these bowls with your favorite toppings, like guacamole, fresh cilantro, and shredded cheese. You can use mild or hot salsa to suit your personal tastes.

2 tablespoons olive oil

1 medium onion, diced

3 garlic cloves, minced

1½ tablespoons chili powder

1½ teaspoons ground cumin

1 cup chicken broth

Salt

Freshly ground black pepper

2 pounds boneless, skinless chicken thighs, cubed

1 (15-ounce) can black beans, drained and rinsed

1 cup frozen corn

1 (16-ounce) jar chunky salsa

1 cup long-grain white rice

1. Turn on the Sauté function, and when the inner pot is hot, pour in the oil. Stir in the onion and garlic and cook until the onion is translucent, about 4 minutes. Add the chili powder and cumin and cook until fragrant, about 1 minute.

2. Add the broth and stir to scrape up the browned bits from the bottom.

3. Evenly sprinkle salt and pepper over the chicken and then place it in the pot. Add the beans, corn, and salsa. Stir well to combine.

4. Sprinkle the rice over the mixture and gently press it down with a spoon to submerge, but do not stir.

5. Lock the lid on the pressure cooker. Set the pressure valve to seal and cook for 10 minutes on manual high pressure. When the time is up, allow for a 5-minute natural release of pressure; then quick release any remaining pressure. Stir everything to combine.

CHICKEN-AND-RICE PORRIDGE

SERVES: 6

PREP TIME: 10 minutes / **SAUTÉ TIME:** 5 minutes / **PRESSURE BUILD:** 20 minutes / **PRESSURE COOK:** 10 minutes / **NATURAL RELEASE:** 25 minutes / **TOTAL TIME:** 1 hour 10 minutes

`NO DIRTY DISHES`

This recipe is inspired by chicken arroz caldo, a thick rice-based porridge that's similar to risotto. Fresh ginger and fish sauce give this dish its unique flavor. To prepare the ginger, use a spoon to gently scrape off the skin.

¼ cup vegetable oil

2 thumbs fresh ginger, peeled and cut into matchsticks

3 garlic cloves, minced

1 large onion, chopped

3 carrots, peeled and cubed

3 celery stalks, sliced

2 tablespoons fish sauce

2 to 3 pounds boneless, skinless chicken thighs

1¼ cups jasmine rice, rinsed

1½ tablespoons salt

1½ teaspoons freshly ground black pepper

2 bay leaves

8 cups chicken broth

6 hard-boiled eggs, peeled, for serving (optional)

Lemon slices, for serving (optional)

1. Turn on the Sauté function, and when the inner pot is hot, pour in the oil. Stir in the ginger, garlic, onion, carrot, and celery and sauté for about 5 minutes, or until the celery is starting to soften. Add the fish sauce and stir.

2. Add the chicken, rice, salt, pepper, bay leaves, and broth. Do not stir.

3. Lock the lid on the pressure cooker. Set the pressure valve to seal and cook for 10 minutes on manual high pressure. When the time is up, allow for a 25-minute natural release of pressure; then quick release any remaining pressure.

4. Remove the chicken and shred it; then stir it back into the pot. Discard the bay leaves. Serve with an egg and slice of lemon (if using).

"DIRTY" RICE

PREP TIME: 10 minutes / **SAUTÉ TIME:** 12 minutes / **PRESSURE BUILD:** 5 minutes / **PRESSURE COOK:** 6 minutes / **NATURAL RELEASE:** 10 minutes / **TOTAL TIME:** 43 minutes

NO DIRTY DISHES

"Dirty" rice is traditionally made with scraps of meat like liver or chicken feet. This version is made with ground beef and Creole seasoning, which gives it a slight kick. I love serving this rice with seafood like steamed clams or grilled shrimp. Turning the pot off while you add the ingredients in step 3 gives it a chance to cool down slightly, helping prevent a burn warning.

1 pound ground beef

½ cup chopped celery

1 small onion, chopped

½ cup chopped green bell pepper

1 cup beef broth

1 tablespoon Creole seasoning

1 teaspoon dried thyme

1 teaspoon dried oregano

Salt

Freshly ground black pepper

1 cup long-grain white rice

1. Turn on the Sauté function, and when the inner pot is hot, put in the beef and brown it, 5 to 7 minutes, breaking up the beef into smaller pieces as it cooks.

2. Add the celery, onion, and bell pepper to the beef and cook until softened, 3 to 5 minutes; then turn off the pressure cooker.

3. Add the beef broth, Creole seasoning, thyme, and oregano and season with salt and pepper, stirring to scrape up all the browned bits from the bottom of the pot. Add the rice; press down with the back of a spoon to submerge, but do not stir.

4. Lock the lid on the pressure cooker. Set the pressure valve to seal and cook for 6 minutes on manual high pressure. When the time is up, allow for a 10-minute natural release of pressure; then quick release any remaining pressure.

5. Fluff the rice with a fork and serve.

CREAMY MAC AND CHEESE
PAGE 68

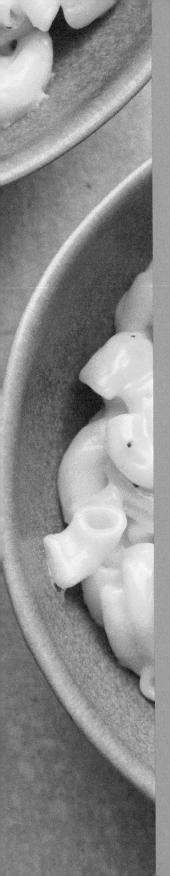

Pasta

CREAMY MAC AND CHEESE

SERVES: 6

PREP TIME: 5 minutes / **PRESSURE BUILD:** 9 minutes / **PRESSURE COOK:** 4 minutes / **QUICK RELEASE** / **TOTAL TIME:** 18 minutes

30 MINUTES OR LESS   NO DIRTY DISHES

This ultra-creamy macaroni and cheese has so much flavor! You'll use the pressure cooker to cook the macaroni and then let the residual heat melt the cheese. If the sauce appears too runny at first, turn on the Sauté function and continually stir the mac and cheese for a minute or two. It will thicken right up.

2½ cups uncooked elbow macaroni

1 cup chicken broth

2 cups water

3 tablespoons unsalted butter, cubed

¼ teaspoon salt

¼ teaspoon freshly ground black pepper

¼ teaspoon mustard powder

¼ teaspoon garlic powder

⅓ cup whole or 2 percent milk

⅓ cup heavy (whipping) cream

2 cups shredded sharp cheddar cheese

1. Combine the macaroni, broth, water, butter, salt, pepper, mustard powder, and garlic powder in the inner pot.

2. Lock the lid on the pressure cooker. Set the pressure valve to seal and cook for 4 minutes on manual high pressure. When the time is up, perform a quick release of pressure.

3. Remove the lid and add the milk, cream, and cheese, stirring until it's smooth and creamy.

VARIATION TIP: Feel free to play with different types of cheese in this recipe. I love using pepper Jack, Gouda, or Gruyère.

CHEESY TUNA NOODLE CASSEROLE

SERVES: 8

PREP TIME: 5 minutes / **SAUTÉ TIME:** 4 minutes / **PRESSURE BUILD:** 9 minutes / **PRESSURE COOK:** 3 minutes / **QUICK RELEASE** / **TOTAL TIME:** 21 minutes

`30 MINUTES OR LESS`   `NO DIRTY DISHES`

For dairy-heavy recipes like this comfort-food classic, take extra care to add the ingredients in the specified order and don't stir them until the final step—this will help prevent a burn warning.

3 tablespoons unsalted butter

1 small onion, diced

3 cups chicken broth

½ teaspoon salt

½ teaspoon freshly ground black pepper

2 garlic cloves, minced

1 teaspoon onion powder

1 cup whole milk

2 (6-ounce) cans chunk white tuna in water, drained

1 (12-ounce) bag frozen peas

12 ounces wide egg noodles, uncooked

2 (10.5-ounce) cans condensed cream of mushroom soup

2 cups shredded mild cheddar cheese

1. Turn on the Sauté function, and when the inner pot is hot, melt the butter. Stir in the onion and cook until translucent, about 4 minutes.

2. Add the broth, salt, pepper, garlic, and onion powder and stir. Then add the milk, tuna, peas, and noodles, but do not stir at this point.

3. Spread the mushroom soup evenly over the noodles. Again, do not stir.

4. Lock the lid on the pressure cooker. Set the pressure valve to seal and cook for 3 minutes on manual high pressure. When the time is up, perform a quick release of pressure. Stir in the cheese and serve.

GO BIG: For the traditional crispy crust, in a small bowl mix together 1 cup of panko bread crumbs, 2 tablespoons of melted butter, and ¾ cup of grated Parmesan cheese. Transfer the cooked casserole to an oven-safe dish, cover with the topping, and broil on high for 2 to 3 minutes, until golden brown.

SHRIMP SCAMPI

SERVE: 6

PREP TIME: 5 minutes / **SAUTÉ TIME:** 5 minutes / **PRESSURE BUILD:** 5 minutes / **PRESSURE COOK:** 5 minutes / **QUICK RELEASE** / **TOTAL TIME:** 20 minutes

30 MINUTES OR LESS   NO DIRTY DISHES

This shrimp scampi cooks with pasta right in the same pot for an easy dinner that's fancy enough to serve company but easy enough for a weeknight.

2 tablespoons olive oil

3 tablespoons unsalted butter

3 garlic cloves, minced

¼ cup finely chopped flat-leaf parsley

½ cup dry white wine (such as Pinot Grigio, Sauvignon Blanc, or Chardonnay)

½ teaspoon red pepper flakes

½ teaspoon salt

½ teaspoon freshly ground black pepper

1 (15-ounce) can chicken broth

Juice of ½ lemon

2 pounds frozen medium shrimp (36–40 count), peeled and deveined

12 ounces angel hair pasta

Lemon wedges, for serving (optional)

1. Turn on the Sauté function and put the oil and butter in the inner pot. When it is hot, stir in the garlic and parsley and cook until fragrant, 1 to 2 minutes. Add the wine, red pepper flakes, salt, and black pepper and cook for about 3 minutes.

2. Add the broth and lemon juice, stirring to scrape up any browned bits from the bottom of the pot.

3. Add the shrimp to the pot. Break the pasta in half and layer it in the pot on top of the shrimp. Make sure the pasta is completely submerged in the liquid. Use tongs to lightly push the pasta down, if necessary, but do not stir.

4. Lock the lid on the pressure cooker. Set the pressure valve to seal and cook for 5 minutes on manual high pressure. When the time is up, perform a quick release of pressure. Stir well and serve with lemon wedges (if using).

BANG BANG SHRIMP PASTA

SERVES: 4

PREP TIME: 5 minutes / **SAUTÉ TIME:** 1 minute / **PRESSURE BUILD:** 10 minutes / **PRESSURE COOK:** 5 minutes / **QUICK RELEASE** / **TOTAL TIME:** 21 minutes

`30 MINUTES OR LESS`

Bang bang sauce is typically served with fried shrimp as an appetizer, but it also makes a rich and creamy accompaniment to pasta.

2 tablespoons olive oil

3 garlic cloves, minced, divided

16 ounces spaghetti, broken in half

3 cups water

1 pound medium shrimp (36–40 count), shells and tails left on

1 teaspoon paprika

¾ tablespoon lime juice

½ cup mayonnaise

⅓ cup Thai sweet chile sauce

2 teaspoons sriracha

¼ teaspoon red pepper flakes

1. Turn on the Sauté function, and when the inner pot is hot, pour in the oil. Stir in the garlic and sauté until fragrant, about 1 minute.

2. Layer the noodles in a crisscross pattern and then add the water. Gently push all the noodles down so that they are covered by water. Put the shrimp in the middle of a piece of aluminum foil. Sprinkle the shrimp with the paprika and lime juice. Fold the foil into a parcel and place it on top of the noodles.

3. Lock the lid on the pressure cooker. Set the pressure valve to seal and cook for 5 minutes on manual high pressure. When the time is up, perform a quick release of pressure.

4. While the pasta is cooking, in a small bowl, mix the mayonnaise, chile sauce, sriracha, and red pepper flakes and set aside.

5. Unfold the shrimp parcel and dump the juices into the pasta. Peel the shrimp and add them to the pasta. Stir well, breaking up any noodle clumps. Stir in the sauce until everything is well combined.

CHICKEN ALFREDO

SERVES: 4

PREP TIME: 5 minutes / **PRESSURE BUILD:** 9 minutes / **PRESSURE COOK:** 5 minutes /
NATURAL RELEASE: 7 minutes / **TOTAL TIME:** 26 minutes

`30 MINUTES OR LESS`   `NO DIRTY DISHES`

Creamy Alfredo sauce is so easy to make in the pressure cooker, and the pasta soaks up so much flavor while it cooks! For the best results, buy a block of Parmesan cheese and grate it yourself. The pre-grated kind is often coated with starch, which can cause the cheese to clump up in the sauce instead of melting smoothly.

1½ cups chicken broth

1½ cups heavy (whipping) cream

3 garlic cloves, minced

Salt

Freshly ground black pepper

8 ounces linguine pasta, broken in half

5 chicken tenderloins

1 cup shredded Parmesan cheese

1. In the order specified, combine the broth, cream, and garlic in the inner pot of your pressure cooker and season with salt and pepper. Layer in the pasta, arranging it in a crisscross pattern to keep it from clumping together. Do not stir, but use the back of a spoon to push the noodles down, ensuring they are covered by the liquids.

2. Place the chicken on the pasta and season with salt and pepper. Lock the lid on the pressure cooker. Set the pressure valve to seal and cook for 5 minutes on manual high pressure. When the time is up, allow for a 7-minute natural release of pressure; then quick release any remaining pressure. Remove the chicken and set aside.

3. Slowly add the Parmesan and stir the pasta around. (Tongs are really helpful here.)

4. Dice the chicken and stir it into the sauce.

BUFFALO CHICKEN PASTA

SERVES: 6

PREP TIME: 5 minutes / **PRESSURE BUILD:** 10 minutes / **PRESSURE COOK:** 14 minutes /
QUICK RELEASE / **TOTAL TIME:** 29 minutes

`30 MINUTES OR LESS`   `NO DIRTY DISHES`

For classic Buffalo flavor, use original Frank's or Texas Pete hot sauce. Be sure not to use wing sauce, which is already flavored with butter.

1 pound boneless, skinless
  chicken breasts

4 tablespoons (½ stick) unsalted butter

1 cup hot sauce

4 cups water, divided

16 ounces penne pasta

8 ounces cream cheese, cubed

1 cup prepared ranch or blue cheese
  dressing

¾ cup shredded Monterey Jack cheese

1. In the inner pot, combine the chicken, butter, hot sauce, and 1 cup of water.

2. Lock the lid on the pressure cooker. Set the pressure valve to seal and cook for 10 minutes on manual high pressure. When the time is up, perform a quick release of pressure. Do not drain the liquid.

3. Transfer the chicken to a plate and shred it.

4. Put the pasta in the pot and lay the shredded chicken on top. Add the cream cheese, dressing, and the remaining 3 cups of water.

5. Lock the lid on the pressure cooker. Set the pressure valve to seal and cook for 4 minutes on manual high pressure. When the time is up, perform a quick release of pressure.

6. Stir in the Monterey Jack cheese and enjoy.

> **GO BIG:** To make this extra indulgent, transfer the cooked pasta and chicken to an oven-safe dish and top with bread crumbs and more shredded cheese. Broil for 1 to 2 minutes, until the top is crispy and golden brown.

GOULASH (OR AMERICAN CHOP SUEY)

SERVES: 6

PREP TIME: 5 minutes / **SAUTÉ TIME:** 7 minutes / **PRESSURE BUILD:** 9 minutes / **PRESSURE COOK:** 5 minutes / **QUICK RELEASE** / **TOTAL TIME:** 26 minutes

30 MINUTES OR LESS   NO DIRTY DISHES

Depending on where you grew up, you likely called this classic dish either gou-lash or American chop suey. Either way, it's a delicious combination of ground beef, macaroni, and savory tomato sauce. When making tomato-based recipes like this one, it's important to add the ingredients in the correct order and not to stir until after they're cooked; otherwise you risk burning.

1 tablespoon oil

1 pound ground beef

1 large onion, chopped

3 garlic cloves, minced

2½ cups water

3 cups elbow noodles, uncooked

2 (15-ounce) cans diced tomatoes

2 (15-ounce) cans tomato sauce

3 tablespoons soy sauce

2 tablespoons Italian seasoning

3 bay leaves

Salt

Freshly ground black pepper

1. Turn on the Sauté function, and when the inner pot is hot, pour in the oil. Add the beef, onion, and garlic and cook until the meat is browned, 5 to 7 minutes.

2. If necessary, drain any fat from the pot. Stir in the water, scraping up any browned bits from the bottom. In the order specified, add the noodles, diced tomatoes and their juices, tomato sauce, soy sauce, Italian seasoning, and bay leaves. Season with salt and pepper. Do not stir.

3. Lock the lid on the pressure cooker. Set the pressure valve to seal and cook for 5 minutes on manual high pressure. When the time is up, perform a quick release of pressure.

4. Remove and discard the bay leaves, and give everything a good stir. If the sauce looks too thin, cover the pot and let it sit for 1 to 2 minutes to thicken.

SPAGHETTI AND MEATBALLS

SERVES: 8

PREP TIME: 5 minutes / **PRESSURE BUILD:** 15 minutes / **PRESSURE COOK:** 3 minutes /
NATURAL RELEASE: 5 minutes / **TOTAL TIME:** 28 minutes

30 MINUTES OR LESS **5 INGREDIENTS OR FEWER** **NO DIRTY DISHES**

*You won't believe how easy it is to make spaghetti and meatballs in your
Instant Pot! Frozen meatballs make this classic meal super simple—you don't
even need to defrost them first. The pasta cooks up perfectly al dente. I actually prefer it to traditionally boiled spaghetti.*

1 (26-ounce) bag Italian-style frozen
    meatballs
16 ounces spaghetti, broken in half

1 (24-ounce) jar pasta sauce
1 cup water
½ cup finely grated Parmesan cheese

1. Add the frozen meatballs to the inner pot. Layer the spaghetti over the
   meatballs in a crisscross pattern. Top with the sauce and water. Do not stir.

2. Lock the lid on the pressure cooker. Set the pressure valve to seal and cook for
   3 minutes on manual high pressure. When the time is up, allow for a 5-minute
   natural release of pressure; then quick release any remaining pressure.

3. Carefully remove the lid and stir everything together. Top with the Parmesan
   and serve immediately.

> **VARIATION TIP:** Jazz this recipe up by adding mushrooms, sliced bell peppers, or
> even pepperoni! Place any additional ingredients directly on top of the meatballs.

ROOT BEER PULLED PORK
PAGE 98

Mains

FRIJOLES BORRACHOS (DRUNKEN BEANS)

SERVES: 8

PREP TIME: 10 minutes / **SAUTÉ TIME:** 12 minutes / **PRESSURE BUILD:** 15 minutes / **PRESSURE COOK:** 22 minutes / **NATURAL RELEASE:** 20 minutes / **TOTAL TIME:** 1 hour 19 minutes

NO DIRTY DISHES

Create a delicious meal from uncooked beans in a little over an hour. This hearty bean recipe is inspired by frijoles borrachos, a classic Mexican dish flavored with earthy spices and malty beer. Serve with rice or tortillas.

¾ pound bacon, diced

1 large onion, diced

2 medium green bell peppers, seeded and diced

5 garlic cloves, minced

1 jalapeño, seeded and diced

1 tablespoon chili powder

1 tablespoon ground cumin

1 teaspoon dried oregano

1 teaspoon salt

1 (12-ounce) Mexican lager beer (such as Modelo)

6 cups chicken broth

2 bay leaves

1 bunch cilantro, tied together for easy removal

1 pound dried pinto beans

1 (14-ounce) can diced tomatoes, with juices

6 cups fully cooked white rice or 6 servings cornbread (optional)

1. Turn on the Sauté function, and when the inner pot is hot, cook the bacon, stirring occasionally, until crisp, 5 to 7 minutes. Remove the bacon and set aside. Discard all but 2 tablespoons of the bacon grease.

2. Add the onion and peppers and cook until the onion is translucent, 4 to 5 minutes. Then add the garlic and jalapeño and cook until fragrant, about 1 minute.

3. Add the chili powder, cumin, oregano, and salt and stir well. Then stir in the beer, broth, bay leaves, cilantro, and beans. Return three-fourths of the cooked bacon to the pot. Add the tomatoes; do not stir.

4. Lock the lid on the pressure cooker. Set the pressure valve to seal and cook for 22 minutes on manual high pressure. When the time is up, allow for a 20-minute natural release of pressure; then quick release any remaining pressure.

5. Open the lid and discard the bay leaves and cilantro. Serve the beans over rice or cornbread.

COOKING TIP: For a faster take on this recipe, you can use three (15.5-ounce) cans of beans (drained and rinsed) in place of the dry beans. Reduce the amount of broth to 1½ cups and cook for 10 minutes under high pressure.

CHICKPEA TIKKA MASALA

SERVES: 6

PREP TIME: 5 minutes / **SAUTÉ TIME:** 13 minutes / **PRESSURE BUILD:** 5 minutes / **PRESSURE COOK:** 2 minutes / **QUICK RELEASE** / **TOTAL TIME:** 25 minutes

`30 MINUTES OR LESS`   `NO DIRTY DISHES`

Garam masala is a spicy curry powder made from peppercorns, cinnamon, cardamom, chili powder, and other spices. Coconut milk will help tame the heat, but this vegetarian dish still has a little bit of a kick. I love serving this chickpea stew over rice or with flatbread like pita or naan.

1 tablespoon unsalted butter

½ cup chopped onion

1 medium red bell pepper, seeded and chopped

2 (15-ounce) cans chopped tomatoes

2 (15-ounce) cans chickpeas, drained

6 garlic cloves, chopped

4 teaspoons garam masala

Salt

Freshly ground black pepper

1 cup full fat coconut milk

4 cups fully cooked white rice (optional)

1. Turn on the Sauté function, and when the inner pot is hot, melt the butter. Stir in the onion and bell pepper and cook until the onion is translucent, about 5 minutes. Add the tomatoes with their juices, chickpeas, garlic, and garam masala, and season with salt and pepper.

2. Lock the lid on the pressure cooker. Set the pressure valve to seal and cook for 2 minutes on manual high pressure. When the time is up, perform a quick release of pressure.

3. Remove the lid and turn the pressure cooker back to the Sauté function. Add the coconut milk and heat until the mixture boils. Serve over rice (if using).

LOW COUNTRY BOIL

SERVE: 6

PREP TIME: 5 minutes / **PRESSURE BUILD:** 10 minutes / **PRESSURE COOK:** 5 minutes /
NATURAL RELEASE: 10 minutes / **TOTAL TIME:** 30 minutes

30 MINUTES OR LESS

Thanks to the Instant Pot, you can enjoy this classic summertime supper year-round! Using frozen shrimp ensures they cook at the same rate as the potatoes and don't come out rubbery and overdone. I like making this recipe with andouille sausage, but any smoked sausage will work.

1½ pounds baby red potatoes

1¼ pounds frozen peel-and-eat shrimp

1 (14-ounce) package smoked sausage,
  cut into 2-inch pieces

3 ears corn, cut into thirds

3 cups water

1 tablespoon Old Bay seasoning

3 teaspoons Creole seasoning, divided

8 tablespoons (1 stick) unsalted butter

½ teaspoon garlic powder

1. Combine the potatoes, shrimp, sausage, and corn in the inner pot. Pour in the water and add the Old Bay seasoning and 2½ teaspoons of Creole seasoning.

2. Lock the lid on the pressure cooker. Set the pressure valve to seal and cook for 5 minutes on manual high pressure. Let the pressure release naturally for 10 minutes; then quick release the remaining pressure.

3. Use a slotted spoon to transfer everything to a serving platter.

4. Meanwhile, in a microwave-safe container, combine the butter and garlic powder. Microwave until the butter is melted. Serve the Low Country boil with the garlic butter as a dipping sauce.

SALMON WITH LEMON BUTTER AND DILL

SERVES: 4

PREP TIME: 5 minutes / **SAUTÉ TIME:** 5 minutes / **PRESSURE BUILD:** 5 minutes / **PRESSURE COOK:** 3 minutes / **QUICK RELEASE** / **TOTAL TIME:** 18 minutes

30 MINUTES OR LESS

Electric pressure cookers are great for cooking fish fillets quickly. Use the trivet to elevate the salmon and keep it out of the cooking liquid. Doing this ensures the fish steams instead of boils.

¾ cup dry white wine

3 tablespoons minced shallot

2 tablespoons lemon juice

8 tablespoons (1 stick) unsalted butter,
   cut into pieces

1½ tablespoons chopped fresh dill

Salt

Freshly ground black pepper

4 (6-ounce) skin-on salmon fillets (¾ to
   1 inch thick)

1 medium lemon, sliced

1. Turn on the Sauté function, and when the inner pot is hot, pour in the white wine and add the shallots and lemon juice. Cook until the shallots are soft, about 3 minutes. Turn off the pressure cooker and add the butter, whisking constantly. When the butter is melted, add the dill and salt and pepper to taste. Transfer the sauce to a bowl and set aside.

2. Set the trivet in the inner pot and pour in 1 cup of water. Place the salmon on the trivet, skin-side down. Sprinkle with salt and pepper and top with the lemon slices.

3. Lock the lid on the pressure cooker. Set the pressure valve to seal, and cook for 3 minutes on manual high pressure. When the time is up, perform a quick release of pressure.

4. Spoon the buttery sauce over the salmon and serve.

> **INGREDIENT TIP:** To cook frozen salmon fillets, increase the cooking time to 5 minutes.

CHICKEN AND GRAVY

SERVES: 4

PREP TIME: 5 minutes / **SAUTÉ TIME:** 8 minutes / **PRESSURE BUILD:** 7 minutes / **PRESSURE COOK:** 5 minutes / **NATURAL RELEASE:** 5 minutes / **TOTAL TIME:** 30 minutes

`30 MINUTES OR LESS`   `5 INGREDIENTS OR FEWER`

Ranch seasoning is my secret ingredient to flavorful chicken that the whole family will love. This savory and tender chicken breast is smothered in a thick gravy that makes it perfect for serving over potatoes, rice, or noodles—or even as a messy but delicious open-faced sandwich over bread.

1 (1-ounce) packet ranch seasoning mix (such as Hidden Valley)

2 pounds boneless, skinless chicken breasts

1 tablespoon olive oil

1½ cups chicken broth

2 tablespoons cornstarch

2 tablespoons cold water

1. Sprinkle the ranch seasoning onto both sides of the chicken. Turn on the Sauté function, and when the inner pot is hot, pour in the oil. Cook the chicken until browned, about 3 minutes per side. Transfer the chicken to a plate.

2. Add the chicken broth to the inner pot and scrape up any browned bits.

3. Place the trivet in the pot and place the chicken on the trivet.

4. Lock the lid on the pressure cooker. Set the pressure valve to seal and cook for 5 minutes on manual high pressure. When the time is up, allow for a 5-minute natural release of pressure; then quick release any remaining pressure.

5. While the chicken is cooking, mix together the cornstarch and cold water to form a slurry.

6. When the cook time is up, remove the chicken and slice it.

7. Turn on the Sauté function and whisk in the slurry. Simmer for a minute or two until it thickens and then turn off the pressure cooker. Serve the gravy over the chicken.

CHICKEN CURRY

SERVES: 4

PREP TIME: 5 minutes / **SAUTÉ TIME:** 15 minutes / **PRESSURE BUILD:** 5 minutes / **PRESSURE COOK:** 5 minutes / **NATURAL RELEASE:** 15 minutes / **TOTAL TIME:** 45 minutes

NO DIRTY DISHES

While many people think curry is a specific recipe, it actually refers to any number of recipes that use a mixture of spices. This Indian-inspired curry has a rich, creamy sauce thanks to the addition of coconut milk. If you like your curries less spicy, leave out the cayenne pepper.

2 pounds boneless, skinless chicken breasts, cubed

Salt

Freshly ground black pepper

2 tablespoons olive oil

1 medium onion, diced

6 garlic cloves, minced

1 tablespoon minced fresh ginger

3 tablespoons curry powder

½ teaspoon cayenne pepper

2 tablespoons tomato paste

1 tablespoon soy sauce

1 cup chicken broth

½ cup coconut milk

1. Dry the chicken thoroughly with paper towels and season with salt and black pepper.

2. Turn on the Sauté function, and when the inner pot is hot, pour in the oil. Place the chicken in the pot and brown on each side for about 4 minutes. Transfer the chicken to a plate and set aside.

3. Add the onion and sauté until beginning to soften, about 3 minutes.

4. Stir in the garlic, ginger, curry powder, cayenne, tomato paste, and soy sauce and sauté for another 2 minutes.

5. Add the chicken broth, stirring to scrape up the browned bits from the bottom of the pot. Return the chicken and any juices to the pot.

6. Lock the lid on the pressure cooker. Set the pressure valve to seal and cook for 5 minutes on manual high pressure. When the time is up, allow for a 15-minute natural release of pressure; then quick release any remaining pressure.

7. Turn the Sauté function back on and add the coconut milk. Cook for about 2 minutes, until warmed through.

VARIATION TIP: I like serving this curry over white or jasmine rice. If you prefer a one-pot meal, add 2 diced russet potatoes and 2 chopped carrots to the pot along with the chicken in step 5. Stir in 1 cup of frozen peas in step 7.

CHICKEN CARNITAS

SERVES: 6

PREP TIME: 10 minutes / **SAUTÉ TIME:** 4 minutes / **PRESSURE BUILD:** 5 minutes / **PRESSURE COOK:** 5 minutes / **NATURAL RELEASE:** 10 minutes / **TOTAL TIME:** 34 minutes

This lighter take on carnitas uses chicken breasts instead of pork and lard. I love serving this in corn tortillas, over nachos, or over rice.

1½ tablespoons ground cumin

1 tablespoon dried oregano

1 teaspoon salt

1 teaspoon freshly ground black pepper

1½ teaspoons chili powder

1 tablespoon olive oil

1 medium onion, chopped

1 garlic clove, minced

¼ cup orange juice

¼ cup lime juice

¼ cup chicken broth

1 pound boneless, skinless
   chicken breasts

1. In a small bowl, mix together the cumin, oregano, salt, pepper, and chili powder. Set aside.

2. Turn on the Sauté function, and when the inner pot is hot, pour in the oil. Stir in the onion and cook until translucent, about 3 minutes. Add the garlic and cook until fragrant, about 1 minute.

3. Add the orange juice, lime juice, chicken broth, and the spice blend. Stir to combine. Add the chicken and press it down lightly into the liquid.

4. Lock the lid on the pressure cooker. Set the pressure valve to seal and cook for 5 minutes on manual high pressure. When the time is up, allow for a 10-minute natural release of pressure; then quick release any remaining pressure.

5. Remove the lid and shred the chicken with a fork. Allow the shredded chicken to soak up the cooking liquid.

COOKING TIP: If you prefer your carnitas crispy, spread the shredded chicken in a single layer on a greased baking sheet and broil on high for 3 to 5 minutes. Toss some of the leftover juice from the pressure cooker over the chicken when it's done.

SAVORY TURKEY BREAST

SERVES: 8

PREP TIME: 15 minutes / **SAUTÉ TIME:** 10 minutes / **PRESSURE BUILD:** 5 minutes / **PRESSURE COOK:** 30 minutes / **NATURAL RELEASE:** 15 minutes / **TOTAL TIME:** 1 hour 15 minutes

Cooking turkey breast in your Instant Pot is a great option when you're low on oven space. Searing the turkey on all sides before cooking it under pressure will ensure it has that classic golden-brown color you'd expect from roast turkey. Serve with Creamy Mashed Potatoes (page 105) for a meal to remember.

3 tablespoons olive oil

1 tablespoon poultry seasoning

1 tablespoon paprika

1 teaspoon garlic powder

1 teaspoon salt

1 teaspoon freshly ground black pepper

½ teaspoon chili powder

½ teaspoon onion powder

½ teaspoon garlic powder

4 pounds boneless turkey breast, thawed if frozen

1 cup chicken broth

2 thyme sprigs

2 tablespoons unsalted butter (optional)

2 tablespoons all-purpose flour (optional)

1. In a small bowl, combine the oil, poultry seasoning, paprika, garlic powder, salt, pepper, chili powder, onion powder, and garlic powder. Pat the turkey breast dry with a paper towel and then coat it all over with the spice mixture.

2. Turn on the Sauté function, and when the inner pot is hot, put the turkey breast in it and brown on all sides, 2 to 3 minutes per side.

3. Remove the turkey breast and set it aside. Add the broth and deglaze the pot, stirring to scrape up the browned bits from the bottom.

4. Add the thyme to the broth and then set the trivet in the pot. Place the turkey on the trivet. Lock the lid on the pressure cooker. Set the pressure valve to seal and cook for 30 minutes on manual high pressure; When the time is

CONTINUED

up, allow for a 15-minute natural release of pressure; then quick release any remaining pressure.

5. Use a meat thermometer to test the temperature of the turkey; make sure it reads 165°F at the thickest part of the breast before removing it from the pot. If it hasn't reached that temperature, close and lock the lid and set the pressure cooker for another 5 to 10 minutes.

6. Transfer the turkey breast to a cutting board and let it rest for 15 minutes before cutting.

7. While the turkey is resting, make the gravy (if using). Scoop out 2 cups of the drippings from the bottom of the pot. Discard the rest, along with the thyme sprigs.

8. Turn the Sauté function back on and add the butter and flour. Whisk constantly for about 1 minute, or until the flour starts to turn golden. Add the drippings and cook until the gravy thickens, 2 to 3 minutes. Adjust the seasoning and transfer to a gravy boat.

9. Slice the turkey breast and serve with the gravy.

COOKING TIP: If you would like a crispy crust on the turkey breast, transfer it to a roasting pan and broil for 6 to 8 minutes, or until the top is golden brown.

STEAMED HAMBURGERS

MAKES: 6

PREP TIME: 10 minutes / **PRESSURE BUILD:** 5 minutes / **PRESSURE COOK:** 15 minutes /
QUICK RELEASE / **TOTAL TIME:** 30 minutes

`30 MINUTES OR LESS`   `5 INGREDIENTS OR FEWER`

I know what you're thinking: hamburgers in a pressure cooker? Trust me on this one. These fast food–style burgers come out so juicy, plus you can make six at a time without babysitting them on the stove! Serve these burgers on soft buns and pile on your favorite toppings.

2 pounds lean ground beef

1 teaspoon salt

½ teaspoon freshly ground black pepper

1 teaspoon garlic powder

2 teaspoons Worcestershire sauce

Cheese slices (optional)

1. In a medium bowl, mix together the beef, salt, pepper, garlic powder, and Worcestershire sauce. Form six thick equal-size patties.

2. Wrap each patty in aluminum foil, carefully sealing all the sides.

3. Set the trivet in the inner pot and pour in 1 cup of water. Stack the burgers evenly on the trivet.

4. Lock the lid on the pressure cooker. Set the pressure valve to seal and cook for 15 minutes on manual high pressure. When the time is up, perform a quick release of pressure.

5. If you want to make cheeseburgers, unwrap the cooked burgers immediately, lay the cheese on top, and allow it to melt.

VARIATION TIP: Try adding finely chopped bacon and shredded cheese to the meat in step 1.

BEEF STROGANOFF

SERVES: 4

PREP TIME: 10 minutes / **SAUTÉ TIME:** 10 minutes / **PRESSURE BUILD:** 5 minutes / **PRESSURE COOK:** 15 minutes / **QUICK RELEASE** / **TOTAL TIME:** 40 minutes

NO DIRTY DISHES

This one-pot beef stroganoff is cooked in two stages. First, you'll cook the beef in the sauce base. Then you'll add the noodles and cook for another few minutes until they're soft.

¼ cup all-purpose flour

Salt

Freshly ground black pepper

2 pounds beef stew meat, cut into bite-size pieces

2 tablespoons unsalted butter

1 small onion, chopped

3 garlic cloves, minced

3 cups sliced baby bella mushrooms

3 cups beef broth

¼ cup cooking sherry

1 tablespoon Worcestershire sauce

1 (12-ounce) package wide egg noodles

8 ounces sour cream

1. In a large resealable plastic bag, mix the flour and salt and pepper to taste. Add the meat and shake until it's evenly coated.

2. Turn on the Sauté function, and when the inner pot is hot, melt the butter. Add the beef and cook for 3 to 5 minutes, or until browned on each side.

3. Add the onion, garlic, and mushrooms and cook until the onion starts to soften, 2 to 4 minutes. Scoop out the beef with a slotted spoon and set aside. Add the broth, sherry, and Worcestershire sauce, stirring to scrape up the browned bits from the bottom of the pot.

4. Return the beef to the pot. Lock the lid on the pressure cooker. Set the pressure valve to seal and cook for 10 minutes on manual high pressure. When the time is up, perform a quick release of pressure.

5. Add the egg noodles; then replace the lid and cook on manual high pressure for an additional 5 minutes. When the time is up, perform a quick release of the pressure.

6. Remove the lid and add the sour cream. Season with salt and pepper. Stir to combine.

SUNDAY POT ROAST

SERVES: 8

PREP TIME: 14 minutes / **SAUTÉ TIME:** 20 minutes / **PRESSURE BUILD:** 6 minutes / **PRESSURE COOK:** 1 hour 10 minutes / **NATURAL RELEASE:** 20 minutes / **TOTAL TIME:** 2 hours 10 minutes

This pot roast recipe uses a two-phase cooking process: Adding the vegetables close to the end of the cooking time will prevent them from overcooking. Don't worry—since the pot is already hot, it will come back to pressure in just a minute or two.

3 pounds beef chuck roast

1 teaspoon kosher salt

1 teaspoon freshly ground black pepper

1 teaspoon dried thyme

1 teaspoon olive oil

1 large onion, chopped

4 garlic cloves, minced

1½ cups beef broth

¾ tablespoon tomato paste

1 tablespoon soy sauce

5 medium carrots, peeled and cut into 1-inch pieces

1½ pounds whole baby potatoes

2 tablespoons cornstarch

2 tablespoons water

1. Cut the roast in half and sprinkle all sides with the salt, pepper, and thyme.

2. Turn on the Sauté function, and when the inner pot is hot, pour in the oil. Place the seasoned meat in the pot and brown all sides, about 4 minutes per side. Transfer the roast to a plate and set aside.

3. Add the onion and cook until translucent, 3 to 5 minutes. Add the garlic and cook until fragrant, about 1 minute.

4. Add the broth and stir to scrape up the browned bits from the bottom of the pot. Add the tomato paste and soy sauce. Return the meat to the pot.

5. Lock the lid on the pressure cooker. Set the pressure valve to seal and cook for 60 minutes on manual high pressure. When the time is up, allow for a 10-minute natural release of pressure; then quick release any remaining pressure.

6. Open the lid and put the carrots and potatoes on top of the meat. Lock the lid on the pressure cooker. Set the pressure valve to seal and cook for 10 minutes on manual high pressure. When the time is up, allow for a 10-minute natural release of pressure; then quick release any remaining pressure.

7. Remove the meat, carrots, and potatoes and shred the meat into large chunks.

8. In a small bowl, make a slurry by mixing together the cornstarch and water. Turn the Sauté function back on and add the slurry to the liquid in the pot. Cook for 2 minutes, stirring often, or until the sauce thickens into gravy.

9. Spoon the gravy over the roast and serve with the potatoes and carrots on the side.

SAUSAGE AND WHITE BEANS

SERVES: 6

PREP TIME: 10 minutes / **SAUTÉ TIME:** 15 minutes / **PRESSURE BUILD:** 20 minutes / **PRESSURE COOK:** 40 minutes / **NATURAL RELEASE:** 15 minutes / **TOTAL TIME:** 1 hour 40 minutes

> NO DIRTY DISHES

This hearty sausage-and-bean stew is a delicious comfort food option that you'll crave all winter long. When cooking with dried beans, keep in mind that older beans can take longer to cook. If they aren't quite done after the initial cooking time, continue to cook under high pressure in 5-minute increments. Also, be sure to check the beans before you add them to the pot and sort out any cracked beans, small stones, or other debris that might have made its way into the bag.

2 teaspoons olive oil

2 pounds sweet Italian sausage

1 large onion, chopped

1 large bay leaf

4 carrots, peeled and chopped (about 1½ cups)

3 celery stalks, chopped (about 1 cup)

4 thyme sprigs or ½ teaspoon dried thyme

1 (4-inch) rosemary sprig

¼ teaspoon dried oregano

4 garlic cloves, pressed or minced

½ teaspoon freshly ground black pepper

6 cups low-sodium chicken broth

3 tablespoons tomato paste

1 pound dried navy beans, rinsed and sorted

1. Turn on the Sauté function and pour in the oil. When hot, add the sausage and cook until lightly browned on all sides, about 6 minutes.

2. Add the onion, bay leaf, carrot, and celery and cook until the onion starts to turn translucent, about 5 minutes. Thoroughly scrape any browned bits from the bottom.

3. Add the thyme, rosemary, oregano, and garlic. Cook until fragrant, about 1 minute.

4. Add the pepper, broth, and tomato paste. Stir and bring to a simmer. Once simmering, add the beans and stir well.

5. Lock the lid on the pressure cooker. Set the pressure valve to seal and cook for 40 minutes on manual high pressure. When the time is up, allow for a 15-minute natural release of pressure; then quick release any remaining pressure.

6. Taste a few beans for tenderness. If not yet tender enough, replace and lock the lid and cook for another 5 minutes. Remove the bay leaf and the thyme and rosemary sprigs and serve.

COOKING TIP: If you want to use canned white beans, rinse and drain them. Add them in step 4 and adjust the broth to 4 cups. The cook time can also be adjusted to 5 minutes with a 10-minute natural release of pressure.

BROWN SUGAR HAM

SERVES: 10

PREP TIME: 5 minutes / **PRESSURE BUILD:** 5 minutes / **PRESSURE COOK:** 10 minutes /
QUICK RELEASE / **TOTAL TIME:** 20 minutes

`30 MINUTES OR LESS`   `5 INGREDIENTS OR FEWER`

Spiral hams are fully cooked during the smoking process, so all you need to do is reheat them. This takes a long time in the oven but is very quick in the pressure cooker! Cooking a ham under pressure also helps the glaze penetrate the meat, giving it so much flavor.

1 (7.5-pound) bone-in spiral ham

1 cup packed light brown sugar

1 cup honey

1 (20-ounce) can pineapple chunks
 in juice

¼ teaspoon ground cloves

1. Place the trivet in the pot and then pour in 1 cup of water. Place the ham on the trivet.

2. In a small bowl, mix together the brown sugar, honey, pineapple, and cloves to form a glaze. Brush the glaze onto the ham.

3. Lock the lid on the pressure cooker. Set the pressure valve to seal and cook for 10 minutes on manual high pressure. When the time is up, perform a quick release of pressure.

4. Slice and serve.

COOKING TIP: For a more browned, caramelized glaze, broil the ham for 3 to 4 minutes before serving. Keep a close eye on it so that it doesn't burn!

SWEET AND SMOKY RIBS

SERVES: 4

PREP TIME: 5 minutes / **PRESSURE BUILD:** 6 minutes / **PRESSURE COOK:** 25 minutes / **NATURAL RELEASE:** 15 minutes / **TOTAL TIME:** 51 minutes

Adding liquid smoke to the cooking liquid gives these ribs that classic grilled-all-day flavor in a fraction of the time. Look for it in small bottles in the spice aisle of your favorite grocery store.

½ cup packed light brown sugar

1½ tablespoons paprika

1 tablespoon garlic powder

1 tablespoon onion powder

1 tablespoon chili powder

1 tablespoon ground cumin

1 teaspoon freshly ground black pepper

2 teaspoons salt

1 rack (1½ to 2 pounds) baby back pork ribs

1½ cups apple juice

1 tablespoon liquid smoke

1 cup barbecue sauce of choice

1. In a small bowl, combine the brown sugar, paprika, garlic powder, onion powder, chili powder, cumin, pepper, and salt to make a dry rub. Mix well.

2. Pat the ribs dry with a paper towel and then remove the thin silvery membrane from the back of the ribs by loosening it with a knife and peeling it off.

3. Generously season both sides of the ribs with the dry rub.

4. Set the trivet in the inner pot and pour in the apple juice and liquid smoke.

5. Add the ribs, standing them vertically and curling them around the pot to fit.

6. Lock the lid on the pressure cooker. Set the pressure valve to seal and cook for 25 minutes on manual high pressure. When the time is up, allow for a 15-minute natural release of pressure; then quick release any remaining pressure.

7. Heat the broiler. Place the ribs on an aluminum foil–lined pan and brush them with the barbecue sauce. Broil for about 3 minutes, or until slightly browned.

ROOT BEER PULLED PORK

SERVES: 8

PREP TIME: 5 minutes / **SAUTÉ TIME:** 20 minutes / **PRESSURE BUILD:** 10 minutes / **PRESSURE COOK:** 50 minutes / **NATURAL RELEASE:** 10 minutes / **TOTAL TIME:** 1 hour 35 minutes

Root beer gives this pulled pork a unique savory flavor. A few dashes of vinegar-based hot sauce, like Tabasco, help balance out the sweetness of the soda. I love serving this on soft rolls or corn tortillas topped with coleslaw.

1 tablespoon salt

1 tablespoon onion powder

1 tablespoon garlic powder

1 tablespoon liquid smoke

1 (4-pound) pork shoulder roast

2 teaspoons olive oil

1 small onion, diced

2 cups root beer soda

1 cup barbecue sauce, plus more for serving

2 or 3 dashes hot sauce

1. In a small dish, mix together the salt, onion powder, garlic powder, and liquid smoke.

2. Pat the pork roast dry with paper towels and cut it into 4 large chunks, trimming off and discarding any large pieces of fat. Season the roast on all sides with the spice mix.

3. Turn on the Sauté function, and when the inner pot is hot, pour in the oil. Sear the pork on all sides, about 3 minutes per side; then transfer it to a plate and set aside. Add the onion to the pot and cook until it starts to turn translucent, 3 to 5 minutes. Press Cancel and allow the pot to cool for 3 to 4 minutes.

4. Return the pork to the pot. In a bowl, mix together the root beer, barbecue sauce, and hot sauce; then pour over the pork.

5. Lock the lid on the pressure cooker. Set the pressure valve to seal and cook for 50 minutes on manual high pressure. When the time is up, allow for a 10-minute natural release of pressure; then quick release any remaining pressure.

6. Remove the pork and shred it with two forks. Spoon ½ cup of the cooking liquid over the pork and allow it to soak in. (Discard the remaining cooking liquid.)

MEXICAN-STYLE STREET CORN SALAD
PAGE 109

BAKED BEANS

SERVES: 12

PREP TIME: 10 minutes / **SAUTÉ TIME:** 13 minutes / **PRESSURE BUILD:** 10 minutes / **PRESSURE COOK:** 60 minutes / **NATURAL RELEASE:** 20 minutes / **TOTAL TIME:** 1 hour 53 minutes

The sauce for these beans will look very thin when you first take the lid off, but don't worry—adding cornstarch will help it thicken into the smooth, glossy sauce you expect.

1 pound thick-cut bacon, chopped

1 cup diced yellow onion

¼ cup apple cider vinegar

1 pound dried navy beans, soaked overnight and drained

4 cups chicken broth

½ cup packed dark brown sugar

⅓ cup ketchup

1 tablespoon Worcestershire sauce

2 teaspoons mustard powder

¼ teaspoon freshly ground black pepper

3 tablespoons cornstarch

½ cup water

1 teaspoon sea salt

1. Turn on the Sauté function and cook the bacon until crispy, about 5 minutes. Add the onion and vinegar. Cook until the onions are translucent and the vinegar is almost evaporated, 3 to 4 minutes. Scrape all the brown bits from the bottom of the pot.

2. Add the drained beans, chicken broth, brown sugar, ketchup, Worcestershire sauce, mustard powder, and pepper and mix well to combine.

3. Lock the lid on the pressure cooker. Set the pressure valve to seal and cook for 60 minutes on manual high pressure. When the time is up, allow for a 20-minute natural release of pressure.

4. In a small bowl, combine the cornstarch and water to make a slurry, mixing until smooth. Switch the pressure cooker back to Sauté and add the cornstarch slurry and salt. Mix well and cook for 3 to 4 minutes, stirring frequently, while the mixture thickens.

5. Turn off the pressure cooker and let the beans sit for 10 minutes before serving.

COOKING TIP: If you don't want to use dried beans, use four 16-ounce cans of navy beans with their liquid and 1 cup of chicken broth. Reduce the cooking time to 5 minutes with a natural pressure release. The beans will be a little lighter but will still have the same great taste.

RESTAURANT-STYLE REFRIED BEANS

SERVES: 6

PREP TIME: 10 minutes / **PRESSURE BUILD:** 15 minutes / **PRESSURE COOK:** 30 minutes / **NATURAL RELEASE:** 10 minutes / **TOTAL TIME:** 1 hour 5 minutes

Soaking the dried beans overnight helps them cook more quickly. If you forgot to soak yours in advance, increase the cooking time to 40 minutes. I like to leave some texture to the beans when mashing them, but for more of a canned style, you can mash until they're completely smooth.

3 cups dried pinto beans, soaked overnight and drained

6 cups chicken broth

1¼ tablespoons ground cumin

¾ teaspoon garlic powder

¾ teaspoon onion powder

1 teaspoon chili powder

1 teaspoon salt

1. Combine the drained beans and broth in the inner pot. Lock the lid on the pressure cooker. Set the pressure valve to seal and cook for 30 minutes on manual high pressure. When the time is up, allow for a 10-minute natural release of pressure; then quick release any remaining pressure.

2. Reserve 1 cup of the bean cooking liquid; then drain the beans.

3. Return ½ cup of the bean cooking liquid to the pot along with the beans. Add the cumin, garlic powder, onion powder, chili powder, and salt. Use an immersion blender (or potato masher) to blend the ingredients. Add more reserved bean liquid to get your desired consistency, if necessary.

MAKE AHEAD: These beans freeze amazingly well. Allow them to fully cool and freeze them in an airtight container for up to 4 months. Thaw them in the refrigerator overnight and reheat either in the microwave or on the stove top.

CREAMY MASHED POTATOES

SERVES: 6

PREP TIME: 5 minutes / **PRESSURE BUILD:** 5 minutes / **PRESSURE COOK:** 10 minutes /
QUICK RELEASE / **TOTAL TIME:** 20 minutes

`30 MINUTES OR LESS` `5 INGREDIENTS OR FEWER`

The pressure cooker makes quick work of mashed potatoes! They'll be ready in under half an hour. For the best results, I like to use starchy potatoes like russet or Yukon gold. When making mashed potatoes, avoid waxy varieties like red or fingerling.

1 cup chicken broth

Salt

3 pounds russet potatoes, peeled and
  quartered

½ cup whole milk

6 tablespoons (¾ stick) unsalted butter,
  at room temperature

1. Set the trivet in the inner pot and pour in the broth and 1 teaspoon of salt. Place the potatoes on the trivet, adding the biggest pieces first so that the others don't fall through.

2. Lock the lid on the pressure cooker. Set the pressure valve to seal and cook for 10 minutes on manual high pressure. When the time is up, perform a quick release of pressure.

3. Remove the lid and then remove the trivet, leaving the potatoes inside the pot.

4. Mash the potatoes with a potato masher and then add the milk and butter. Continue to mash until all the lumps have been removed, and season with additional salt if desired.

COOKING TIP: For a smoother consistency, blend the potatoes with a hand mixer until smooth. Do not use an immersion blender, or the potatoes will come out gummy.

POTATO SALAD

SERVES: 8

PREP TIME: 10 minutes / **PRESSURE BUILD:** 10 minutes / **PRESSURE COOK:** 4 minutes /
QUICK RELEASE / **TOTAL TIME:** 24 minutes, plus 1 hour to chill

*Cooking the potatoes and eggs together in the pressure cooker makes easy
work of this traditional Southern-style potato salad.*

8 medium russet potatoes, peeled and
   cut into 1-inch cubes

2 tablespoons distilled white vinegar

4 cups water

1 tablespoon salt

4 large eggs

1¼ cups mayonnaise

1 tablespoon prepared mustard

2 tablespoons sweet pickle relish

½ teaspoon freshly ground black pepper

1 small onion, diced

½ teaspoon paprika

1. Combine the potatoes, vinegar, water, and salt in the inner pot. Place the eggs on top of the potatoes. Fill a bowl with ice water.

2. Lock the lid on the pressure cooker. Set the pressure valve to seal and cook for 4 minutes on manual high pressure. When the time is up, perform a quick release of pressure.

3. Remove the lid and place the eggs in the ice bath; then drain the potatoes.

4. In a large bowl, mix together the mayonnaise, mustard, relish, and pepper.

5. Remove the eggs from the ice bath; then peel and chop them.

6. Add the potatoes, eggs, and onion to the bowl with the dressing. Mix everything until well combined. Sprinkle with the paprika. Refrigerate the potato salad for at least 1 hour before serving.

MAKE AHEAD: This will keep in a tightly sealed container in the refrigerator for up to 4 days.

SWEET POTATO CASSEROLE

SERVES: 6

PREP TIME: 10 minutes / **PRESSURE BUILD:** 5 minute / **PRESSURE COOK:** 14 minutes / **NATURAL RELEASE:** 15 minutes / **TOTAL TIME:** 44 minutes

These light and fluffy sweet potatoes are a classic for Thanksgiving. If you don't have a hand mixer, you can use a potato masher or even a heavy spoon to mash the potatoes, but they won't be as fluffy.

2 pounds sweet potatoes, washed and cut in half lengthwise

4 tablespoons (½ stick) unsalted butter

2 tablespoons dark brown sugar

⅔ cup heavy cream, plus more if needed

½ teaspoon salt

2 teaspoons ground cinnamon

½ teaspoon ground nutmeg

Mini marshmallows (optional)

Walnuts (optional)

1. Set the trivet in the inner pot and pour in 1 cup of water. Place the sweet potatoes, cut-side up, on the trivet, stacking them if needed.

2. Lock the lid on the pressure cooker. Set the pressure valve to seal and cook for 14 minutes on manual high pressure. When the time is up, allow for a 15-minute natural release of pressure; then quick release any remaining pressure.

3. Remove the lid and trivet and drain the water. Turn on the Sauté function and scoop the sweet potato flesh into the inner pot.

4. Add the butter, brown sugar, cream, salt, cinnamon, and nutmeg. Mash the potatoes with a hand mixer and stir everything to combine.

5. Turn off the pressure cooker and top the sweet potatoes with mini marshmallows and walnuts (if using). Return the cover to the pot and let sit for 2 to 3 minutes for the marshmallows to soften.

COLLARD GREENS

SERVES: 6

PREP TIME: 5 minutes / **PRESSURE BUILD:** 10 minutes / **PRESSURE COOK:** 60 minutes /
QUICK RELEASE / **TOTAL TIME:** 1 hour 15 minutes

`5 INGREDIENTS OR FEWER` `NO DIRTY DISHES`

*Collard greens can be tough, but cooking them under pressure softens them up
perfectly. You can find whole smoked turkey legs in most major grocery stores;
they add a ton of flavor to these tasty greens.*

1 smoked turkey leg (or ham hock)

3 garlic cloves, minced

5 cups chicken broth

1 (2-pound) bag fresh collard greens

¼ teaspoon red pepper flakes

1. Combine all the ingredients in the inner pot. You may need to pack in the
   collard greens.

2. Lock the lid on the pressure cooker. Set the pressure valve to seal and cook
   for 60 minutes on manual high pressure (50 minutes if you prefer a firmer
   bite to the greens). When the time is up, perform a quick release of pressure.

3. Remove the turkey leg and shred the meat, discarding the bones and skin.
   Return the meat to the greens, stir well, and serve.

INGREDIENT TIP: If you can't find smoked turkey legs, you can use ½ to 1 pound of
cooked bacon.

MEXICAN-STYLE STREET CORN SALAD

SERVES: 10

PREP TIME: 5 minutes / **SAUTÉ TIME:** 8 minutes / **PRESSURE BUILD:** 5 minutes / **PRESSURE COOK:** 2 minutes / **QUICK RELEASE** / **TOTAL TIME:** 20 minutes

30 MINUTES OR LESS   **NO DIRTY DISHES**

This salad is a delicious twist on the oh-so-popular Mexican street corn. It has all the delicious taste while turning it into a convenient salad that's great for any party or barbecue.

2 tablespoons olive oil

1 cup frozen white and gold corn

1 cup frozen yellow corn

1 small onion, diced

1 jalapeño, seeded and diced

½ cup water

2 garlic cloves, minced

½ teaspoon paprika

½ teaspoon chili powder

½ teaspoon ground cumin

½ teaspoon salt

¼ teaspoon freshly ground black pepper

3 ounces cream cheese, at room temperature

Juice of 1 to 2 limes

½ cup cotija cheese or queso fresco

1. Turn on the Sauté function, and when the inner pot is hot, pour in the oil. Add all the frozen corn and cook for 3 minutes while stirring.

2. Add the onion and jalapeño and cook until the onion turns translucent, 3 to 5 minutes.

3. Add the water, garlic, paprika, chili powder, cumin, salt, and pepper.

4. Lock the lid on the pressure cooker. Set the pressure valve to seal and cook for 2 minutes on manual high pressure. When the time is up, perform a quick release of pressure.

5. Take off the lid and add the cream cheese, stirring until it's melted; then add the lime juice to taste.

6. Spoon into bowls and top with the cheese.

CORN ON THE COB

SERVES: 6

PREP TIME: 5 minutes / **PRESSURE BUILD:** 10 minutes / **PRESSURE COOK:** 2 minutes /
QUICK RELEASE / **TOTAL TIME:** 17 minutes

`30 MINUTES OR LESS` `5 INGREDIENTS OR FEWER` `NO DIRTY DISHES`

*Cooking this corn under pressure infuses each kernel with butter and cream.
It's so sweet and juicy that you'll never want to make corn any other way!*

4 cups water

½ cup heavy (whipping) cream or 1 cup
  half-and-half

4 tablespoons (½ stick) unsalted butter

6 ears corn, shucked and halved
  crosswise

1. Combine the water, cream, and butter in the inner pot and stir well. Then place the corn in the pot, standing the cobs vertically to fit.

2. Lock the lid on the pressure cooker. Set the pressure valve to seal and cook for 2 minutes on manual high pressure. When the time is up, perform a quick release of pressure.

3. Remove the corn and let it sit for 5 minutes before serving.

COOKING TIP: You can reuse the same cooking liquid to make more corn if you want. The cooking time will stay the same, but the pressure will build much more quickly.

S'MORES PIE
PAGE 124

Dessert

RICE PUDDING

SERVES: 8

PREP TIME: 5 minutes / **SAUTÉ TIME:** 7 minutes / **PRESSURE BUILD:** 7 minutes / **PRESSURE COOK:** 13 minutes / **QUICK RELEASE** / **TOTAL TIME:** 32 minutes

NO DIRTY DISHES

Thick and creamy rice pudding is such a treat! Serve it warm straight from the pot or chill it overnight. It's very important to use whole milk for this recipe. Reduced fat or skim milk won't set up the same way, so the pudding won't have the right texture.

1 cup Arborio rice

1½ cups water

¼ teaspoon kosher salt

2 cups whole milk, divided

½ cup sugar

2 large eggs, beaten

1 teaspoon vanilla extract

1 cup raisins (optional)

1. Combine the rice, water, and salt in the inner pot. Stir well.

2. Lock the lid on the pressure cooker. Set the pressure valve to seal and cook for 13 minutes on manual high pressure. When the time is up, perform a quick release of pressure.

3. Add 1½ cups of milk and the sugar and stir to combine.

4. Turn on the Sauté function and stir in the eggs, the remaining ½ cup of milk, and the vanilla. Cook until the rice pudding starts to boil and then turn off the pressure cooker. Stir in the raisins (if using), and serve.

COOKING TIP: For extra flavor, sprinkle your dish with a dusting of cinnamon or cardamom.

BAKED APPLES

SERVES: 6

PREP TIME: 15 minutes / **PRESSURE BUILD:** 5 minutes / **PRESSURE COOK:** 5 minutes /
QUICK RELEASE / **TOTAL TIME:** 25 minutes

30 MINUTES OR LESS

These soft apples are stuffed with a sweet combination of oats and spices. To prevent the filling from falling through the bottom of the apples and burning, be sure not to cut all the way through the apples when removing their cores.

¾ cup old-fashioned oats

¼ teaspoon ground cinnamon

¼ teaspoon ground nutmeg

½ teaspoon ground allspice

⅓ cup packed light brown sugar

3 tablespoons salted butter, melted

6 apples, cored

1. In a medium bowl, mix together the oats, cinnamon, nutmeg, allspice, and brown sugar. Add the melted butter and stir until well combined.

2. Fill the core of each apple with about 2 tablespoons of the oat mixture, using it all.

3. Set the trivet in the inner pot and pour in 1 cup of water. Place the apples on the trivet carefully so that they fit next to each other; then lock the lid on the pressure cooker. Set the pressure valve to seal and cook for 5 minutes on manual high pressure. When the time is up, perform a quick release of pressure.

4. Carefully remove each apple, place on a plate, and serve.

APPLE CRISP

SERVES: 5

PREP TIME: 10 minutes / **PRESSURE BUILD:** 8 minutes / **PRESSURE COOK:** 5 minutes /
NATURAL RELEASE: 10 minutes / **TOTAL TIME:** 33 minutes

*Use firm baking apples, such as Granny Smith, Honey Crisp, or Pink Lady, for
this recipe. Softer apples will cook down into an applesauce-like mush.*

5 Granny Smith apples (or another firm
  variety), peeled, cored, and cubed

¾ teaspoon ground nutmeg

2 teaspoons ground cinnamon

1 tablespoon pure maple syrup

2 tablespoons caramel sauce

½ cup water

4 tablespoons (½ stick) salted
  butter, melted

¼ cup all-purpose flour

⅓ cup packed light brown sugar

½ teaspoon sea salt

¾ cup old-fashioned oats

1. Combine the apples, nutmeg, cinnamon, maple syrup, caramel sauce, and
   water in the inner pot and stir well.

2. In a small bowl, mix together the melted butter, flour, brown sugar, salt, and
   oats. Sprinkle the topping mix over the apples.

3. Lock the lid on the pressure cooker. Set the pressure valve to seal and cook
   for 5 minutes on manual high pressure. When the time is up, allow for a
   10-minute natural release of pressure; then quick release any remaining pressure.

4. Scoop and serve hot right from the pressure cooker.

PEACH COBBLER

SERVES: 4

PREP TIME: 5 minutes / **PRESSURE BUILD:** 5 minutes / **PRESSURE COOK:** 15 minutes /
NATURAL RELEASE: 10 minutes / **TOTAL TIME:** 35 minutes

5 INGREDIENTS OR FEWER

*Dry yellow cake mix combined with melted butter makes the perfect
dumpling-like topping for this cobbler. Feel free to use fresh or frozen peaches
for this recipe. If using frozen, there is no need to defrost beforehand.*

Nonstick cooking spray

1 (15.25-ounce) box yellow cake mix

8 tablespoons (1 stick) unsalted
  butter, melted

½ teaspoon ground cinnamon

4 cups sliced peaches

1 teaspoon cornstarch

1. Spray a 7-inch cake pan with cooking spray.

2. In a medium bowl, combine the cake mix, melted butter, and cinnamon.
    The mixture will be stiff and hard to stir, but don't worry—that's how it's
    supposed to be.

3. Add the sliced peaches to the prepared pan. Sprinkle with the cornstarch
    and mix well. Spread the cake mixture over the top; then wrap the whole
    pan in foil.

4. Set the trivet in the inner pot and pour in 1 cup of water. Place the pan
    on the trivet.

5. Lock the lid on the pressure cooker. Set the pressure valve to seal and cook
    for 15 minutes on manual high pressure. When the time is up, allow for
    a 10-minute natural release of pressure; then quick release any remain-
    ing pressure.

KEY LIME PIE

SERVES: 6

PREP TIME: 20 minutes / **PRESSURE BUILD:** 5 minutes / **PRESSURE COOK:** 15 minutes / **NATURAL RELEASE:** 10 minutes / **TOTAL TIME:** 50 minutes, plus 4 hours to chill

This tart, creamy pie is delicious on hot summer nights. Be sure to use key lime juice, which is much sweeter and has a different flavor than regular lime juice. If you can't find fresh key limes, bottled juice is available in most major grocery stores.

Nonstick cooking spray

1 cup graham cracker crumbs (about 5 crackers)

3 tablespoons unsalted butter, melted

1 tablespoon sugar

4 large egg yolks

1 (14-ounce) can sweetened condensed milk

½ cup key lime juice

⅓ cup sour cream

2 tablespoons grated key lime zest

Whipped cream, for topping

1. Spray a 7-inch springform pan with cooking spray.

2. In a small bowl, mix together the graham cracker crumbs, melted butter, and sugar. Using the bottom of a measuring cup, evenly press the mixture into the bottom of the prepared pan and up the sides. Place in the freezer for 10 to 15 minutes.

3. In a large bowl, beat the egg yolks until they are light yellow. Slowly add the condensed milk and continue to stir until thickened. Add the lime juice, sour cream, and lime zest and stir until smooth. Pour the mixture into the springform pan, smooth the top, and cover the pan with aluminum foil.

4. Set the trivet in the inner pot and pour in 1 cup of water. Carefully place the pan on the trivet.

5. Lock the lid on the pressure cooker. Set the pressure valve to seal and cook for 15 minutes on manual high pressure. When the time is up, allow for a 10-minute natural release of pressure; then quick release any remaining pressure.

6. Remove the pie and check to see if the middle is set (or slightly firm). If not, cover it back up and cook for an additional 5 minutes.

7. Set the pie on a rack to cool and remove the foil. When the pie is cooled, refrigerate it for at least 4 hours or overnight. Top with whipped cream and enjoy.

CHOCOLATE CHIP BANANA BREAD

SERVES: 6

PREP TIME: 10 minutes / **PRESSURE BUILD:** 5 minutes / **PRESSURE COOK:** 50 minutes / **NATURAL RELEASE:** 10 minutes / **TOTAL TIME:** 1 hour 15 minutes

Covering this banana bread with a layer of paper towel and aluminum foil helps trap condensation as it cooks, resulting in a beautifully browned top. Don't be tempted to skip this step or your bread can come out soggy.

Nonstick cooking spray

8 tablespoons (1 stick) unsalted butter, at room temperature

½ cup packed light brown sugar

2 large eggs, at room temperature

1 teaspoon vanilla extract

2 very ripe bananas, mashed

2 cups all-purpose flour

1½ teaspoons baking soda

½ teaspoon salt

½ teaspoon ground cinnamon

½ cup semisweet chocolate chips

1. Spray a 7-inch cake pan with cooking spray.

2. In a large bowl and using a hand mixer, cream the butter and sugar together. Add the eggs and vanilla and mix to combine. Add the bananas and blend until just combined.

3. In a separate bowl, mix together the flour, baking soda, salt, and cinnamon.

4. Pour the dry ingredients into the wet ingredients and stir them together until you see no more streaks of flour. Stir in the chocolate chips until combined.

5. Pour the batter into the prepared pan, smooth the top, cover the pan loosely with a paper towel, and then wrap it in aluminum foil.

6. Set the trivet in the inner pot and pour in 1 cup of water. Place the pan on the trivet.

7. Lock the lid on the pressure cooker. Set the pressure valve to seal and cook for 50 minutes on manual high pressure. When the time is up, allow for a 10-minute natural release of pressure; then quick release any remaining pressure.

8. Remove the foil and let the bread sit for at least 10 minutes before slicing.

INGREDIENT TIP: For the best banana flavor, choose very ripe bananas with a lot of brown on their peels. They're sweeter and have a stronger flavor than bananas with more yellow or green peels.

LEMON-LIME BUNDT CAKE

SERVES: 6

PREP TIME: 5 minutes / **PRESSURE BUILD:** 5 minutes / **PRESSURE COOK:** 45 minutes /
QUICK RELEASE / **TOTAL TIME:** 55 minutes

5 INGREDIENTS OR FEWER

*The carbonation in soda helps this cake rise, giving it a delicate texture that
you'll love.*

Nonstick cooking spray

1 (15.25-ounce) box yellow cake mix

¾ cup lemon-lime soda

¾ cup vegetable oil

4 large eggs

1. Spray a 7-inch Bundt pan with cooking spray.

2. In a medium bowl, mix together the cake mix, soda, oil, and eggs.

3. Pour the mixture into the prepared Bundt pan.

4. Set the trivet in the inner pot and pour in 1 cup of water. Place the Bundt pan
   on the trivet.

5. Lock the lid on the pressure cooker. Set the pressure valve to seal and cook
   for 45 minutes on manual high pressure. When the time is up, perform a
   quick release of pressure.

6. Let the cake cool slightly before serving.

GO BIG: You can make a delicious glaze for this cake by combining 2 cups of pow-
dered sugar, 2 tablespoons of melted unsalted butter, 1 teaspoon of grated lemon
zest, and 3 to 4 tablespoons of whole milk (depending on how thick you want the
glaze). Let the cake cool for at least 15 minutes before drizzling it with the glaze.

CRÈME BRÛLÉE

SERVES: 6

PREP TIME: 15 minutes / **PRESSURE BUILD:** 5 minutes / **PRESSURE COOK:** 10 minutes /
NATURAL RELEASE: 15 minutes / **TOTAL TIME:** 45 minutes, plus 4 hours to chill

5 INGREDIENTS OR FEWER

Cooking crème brûlée under pressure ensures it comes out perfectly creamy and evenly cooked every time. Be sure to plan ahead, since this will need to chill for at least 4 hours before serving.

6 tablespoons granulated sugar, plus
   4½ teaspoons, for topping
6 large egg yolks

2 cups heavy (whipping) cream
1½ teaspoons vanilla extract
⅛ teaspoon salt

1. In a medium bowl, whisk together 6 tablespoons of sugar and the egg yolks. While whisking constantly, add the cream, vanilla, and salt. Pour the mixture through a fine-mesh strainer.

2. Divide and fill six 6-ounce ramekins three-fourths full and then remove any air bubbles with the back of a spoon. Cover each ramekin tightly with aluminum foil.

3. Set the trivet in the inner pot and pour in 1 cup of water. Place 4 ramekins on the trivet and stack the remaining 2 on top.

4. Lock the lid on the pressure cooker. Set the pressure valve to seal and cook for 10 minutes on manual low pressure. When the time is up, allow for a 15-minute natural release of pressure; then quick release any remaining pressure.

5. Carefully transfer the ramekins to a baking sheet and let cool at room temperature for 30 minutes. Refrigerate until chilled, at least 4 hours and up to overnight.

6. Spread ¾ teaspoon of sugar evenly on top of each cooked crème brûlée. Use a kitchen torch to caramelize the sugar and make a crispy top. Let them sit for 5 minutes before serving.

S'MORES PIE

SERVES: 6

PREP TIME: 10 minutes / **PRESSURE BUILD:** 5 minutes / **PRESSURE COOK:** 45 minutes /
NATURAL RELEASE: 10 minutes / **TOTAL TIME:** 1 hour 10 minutes, plus 30 minutes to cool

This layered dessert includes all of the flavors of s'mores, right down to the gooey marshmallows. Using boxed brownie mix is a nice shortcut to keep things simple. The amount of oil, water, and egg you need to prepare the mix can differ depending on which brand you buy, so be sure to follow the instructions on the box.

Nonstick cooking spray

1 cup graham cracker crumbs (about
  5 crackers)

4 tablespoons (½ stick) unsalted
  butter, melted

1 (18-ounce) box brownie mix

1 egg

½ cup vegetable oil

⅓ cup water

4 whole graham crackers

⅔ cup marshmallow fluff

1 cup mini marshmallows

1. Spray a 7-inch springform pan with cooking spray.

2. In a small bowl, combine the graham cracker crumbs and melted butter. Scrape the mixture into the prepared pan and use the bottom of a measuring cup to evenly press the mixture on the bottom of the pan and about 1 inch up the sides.

3. In a mixing bowl, combine the brownie mix, egg, oil, and water as instructed on the box.

4. Pour half of the prepared brownie batter into the bottom of the pan and then place the whole graham crackers on top. You can break them up to fit if necessary.

5. Spread the marshmallow fluff gently over the graham crackers and then carefully top with the remaining brownie batter. Cover the pan tightly with aluminum foil.

6. Set the trivet in the inner pot and pour in 1 cup of water. Place the covered pan on the trivet.

7. Lock the lid on the pressure cooker. Set the pressure valve to seal and cook for 45 minutes on manual high pressure. When the time is up, allow for a 10-minute natural release of pressure; then quick release any remaining pressure.

8. Heat the broiler. Uncover the cake and place the mini marshmallows in an even layer on top. Broil for 3 to 5 minutes, until golden brown. Alternatively, use a kitchen torch and skip the broiling.

9. Allow the pie to cool for 20 to 30 minutes before serving.

FUDGY BROWNIE BITES

MAKES 7 BITES

PREP TIME: 5 minutes / **PRESSURE BUILD:** 5 minutes / **PRESSURE COOK:** 22 minutes /
NATURAL RELEASE: 25 minutes / **TOTAL TIME:** 57 minutes

5 INGREDIENTS OR FEWER

*Making these brownie bites in a pressure cooker instead of the oven keeps
them super rich and fudgy. Feel free to swap the walnuts for your favorite
nuts or leave them out.*

Nonstick cooking spray

¼ cup diced walnuts

¼ cup hot fudge sauce

1 (10.25-ounce) pouch brownie mix

1 egg

⅓ cup vegetable oil

2 tablespoons water

1. Spray a 7-cup silicone egg bite mold with cooking spray.

2. Evenly divide and sprinkle the walnuts in the cups of the egg mold and then drizzle each with the hot fudge.

3. In a mixing bowl, combine the brownie mix, egg, oil, and water as instructed on the pouch.

4. Spoon the prepared batter into the egg bite mold until each cup is about three-fourths full and then cover the mold with aluminum foil.

5. Set the trivet in the inner pot and pour in 1 cup of water. Place the egg bite mold on the trivet.

6. Lock the lid on the pressure cooker. Set the pressure valve to seal and cook for 22 minutes on manual high pressure. When the time is up, allow for a 25-minute natural release of pressure.

7. Take the mold out and then remove the foil. Allow the brownies to cool completely before popping them out.

GO BIG: Top these brownie bites with a drizzle of caramel and a scoop of ice cream to turn them into a turtle brownie sundae.

USING THE INSTANT POT AT HIGH ALTITUDES

Air pressure is lower at high elevations. This reduces the boiling point of water, meaning that food will be cooking at a lower temperature. To account for this, increase the cooking time by 5 percent for every 1,000 feet above 2,000 feet in elevation.

For example, Denver is a little over 5,200 feet in elevation, so if you live there, you'll need to increase cooking time by 15 percent. That means a recipe that typically needs 20 minutes of cooking time would need to cook for 23 minutes.

Some newer Instant Pot models, like the Ultra and Max, can be programmed to make these time adjustments automatically. Press the center dial to change the system-level settings, and then rotate the dial to "Alt." Enter your altitude and hit Start to save. Once this adjustment has been made, you can follow the recipe instructions as written without making manual adjustments.

INSTANT POT PRESSURE COOKING TIMETABLES

The following charts provide approximate times for a variety of foods. To begin, you may want to cook for a minute or two less than the times listed; if necessary, you can always simmer foods for a few minutes to finish cooking.

Keep in mind that these times are for foods partially submerged in water (or broth) or steamed and are for the foods cooked alone. The cooking times for the same foods may vary if additional ingredients or cooking liquids are added or a different release method than the one listed here is used.

For any foods labeled with "natural" release, allow at least 15 minutes natural pressure release before quick releasing any remaining pressure.

BEANS AND LEGUMES

When cooking 1 pound or more of dried beans, it's best to use low pressure and increase the cooking time by a minute or two. You can add a little oil to the cooking liquid to help reduce foaming. Unless a shorter release time is indicated, let the beans release naturally for at least 15 minutes, after which any remaining pressure can be quick released. Beans should be soaked in salted water for 8 to 24 hours.

	LIQUID PER 1 CUP OF BEANS	MINUTES UNDER PRESSURE	PRESSURE	RELEASE
BLACK BEANS	2 cups	8	High	Natural
		9	Low	
BLACK-EYED PEAS	2 cups	5	High	Natural for 8 minutes, then quick
BROWN LENTILS (UNSOAKED)	2¼ cups	20	High	Natural for 10 minutes, then quick
CANNELLINI BEANS	2 cups	5	High	Natural
		7	Low	
CHICKPEAS (GARBANZO BEANS)	2 cups	4	High	Natural for 3 minutes, then quick
KIDNEY BEANS	2 cups	5	High	Natural
		7	Low	
LIMA BEANS	2 cups	4	High	Natural for 5 minutes, then quick
		5	Low	
PINTO BEANS	2 cups	8	High	Natural
		10	Low	
RED LENTILS (UNSOAKED)	3 cups	10	High	Natural for 5 minutes, then quick
SOYBEANS, DRIED	2 cups	12	High	Natural
		14	Low	
SOYBEANS, FRESH (EDAMAME, UNSOAKED)	1 cup	1	High	Quick
SPLIT PEAS (UNSOAKED)	3 cups	5 (firm peas) to 8 (soft peas)	High	Natural

GRAINS

Thoroughly rinse grains before cooking or add a small amount of butter or oil to the cooking liquid to prevent foaming. Unless a shorter release time is indicated, let the grains release naturally for at least 15 minutes, after which any remaining pressure can be quick released.

	LIQUID PER 1 CUP OF GRAIN	MINUTES UNDER PRESSURE	PRESSURE	RELEASE
ARBORIO RICE (FOR RISOTTO)	3–4 cups	6–8	High	Quick
BARLEY, PEARLED	2½ cups	20	High	Natural for 10 minutes, then quick
BROWN RICE, LONG GRAIN	1 cup	22	High	Natural for 10 minutes, then quick
BROWN RICE, MEDIUM GRAIN	1 cup	12	High	Natural
BUCKWHEAT	1¾ cups	2–4	High	Natural
FARRO, PEARLED	2 cups	6–8	High	Natural
FARRO, WHOLE GRAIN	3 cups	22–24	High	Natural
OATS, ROLLED	3 cups	3–4	High	Quick
OATS, STEEL CUT	3 cups	10	High	Natural for 10 minutes, then quick
QUINOA	1 cup	2	High	Natural for 12 minutes, then quick
WHEAT BERRIES	2 cups	30	High	Natural for 10 minutes, then quick
WHITE RICE, LONG GRAIN	1 cup	3	High	Natural
WILD RICE	1¼ cups	22–24	High	Natural

MEAT

Except as noted, these times are for braised meats—that is, meats that are seared and then pressure cooked while partially submerged in liquid. Unless a shorter release time is indicated, let the meat release naturally for at least 15 minutes, after which any remaining pressure can be quick released.

	MINUTES UNDER PRESSURE	PRESSURE	RELEASE
BEEF, BONE-IN SHORT RIBS	40	High	Natural
BEEF, FLAT IRON STEAK, CUT INTO ½-INCH STRIPS	6	Low	Quick
BEEF, SHOULDER (CHUCK), 2-INCH CHUNKS	20	High	Natural for 10 minutes
BEEF, SHOULDER (CHUCK) ROAST (2 LB.)	35–45	High	Natural
BEEF, SIRLOIN STEAK, CUT INTO ½-INCH STRIPS	3	Low	Quick
LAMB, SHANKS	40	High	Natural
LAMB, SHOULDER, 2-INCH CHUNKS	35	High	Natural
PORK, BACK RIBS (STEAMED)	25	High	Quick
PORK, SHOULDER, 2-INCH CHUNKS	20	High	Quick
PORK, SHOULDER ROAST (2 LB.)	25	High	Natural
PORK, SMOKED SAUSAGE, ½-INCH SLICES	5–10	High	Quick
PORK, SPARE RIBS (STEAMED)	20	High	Quick
PORK, TENDERLOIN	4	Low	Quick

POULTRY

Except as noted, these times are for braised poultry—that is, partially submerged in liquid. Unless a shorter release time is indicated, let the poultry release naturally for at least 15 minutes, after which any remaining pressure can be quick released.

	MINUTES UNDER PRESSURE	PRESSURE	RELEASE
CHICKEN BREAST, BONE-IN (STEAMED)	8	Low	Natural for 5 minutes
CHICKEN BREAST, BONELESS (STEAMED)	5	Low	Natural for 8 minutes
CHICKEN THIGH, BONE-IN	10–14	High	Natural for 10 minutes
CHICKEN THIGH, BONELESS	6–8	High	Natural for 10 minutes
CHICKEN THIGH, BONELESS, 1- TO 2-INCH PIECES	5–6	High	Quick
CHICKEN, WHOLE (SEARED ON ALL SIDES)	12–14	Low	Natural for 8 minutes
DUCK QUARTERS, BONE-IN	35	High	Quick
TURKEY BREAST, TENDERLOIN (12 OZ.) (STEAMED)	5	Low	Natural for 8 minutes
TURKEY THIGH, BONE-IN	30	High	Natural

FISH AND SEAFOOD

All times are for steamed fish and shellfish. Use the trivet to lift the fish/seafood above the cooking liquid so that it steams instead of boils.

	MINUTES UNDER PRESSURE	PRESSURE	RELEASE
CLAMS	2	High	Quick
HALIBUT, FRESH (1-INCH THICK)	3	High	Quick
LARGE SHRIMP, FROZEN	1	Low	Quick
MUSSELS	1	High	Quick
SALMON, FRESH (1-INCH THICK)	5	Low	Quick
TILAPIA OR COD, FRESH	1	Low	Quick
TILAPIA OR COD, FROZEN	3	Low	Quick

VEGETABLES

The following cooking times are for steamed vegetables; if the vegetables are submerged in liquid, the times may vary. Green vegetables will be tender-crisp; root vegetables will be soft. Most vegetables require a quick release of pressure to stop the cooking process; for those that indicate a natural release, let the pressure release for at least 15 minutes, after which any remaining pressure can be quick released.

	PREP	MINUTES UNDER PRESSURE	PRESSURE	RELEASE
ACORN SQUASH	Halved	9	High	Quick
ARTICHOKES, LARGE	Whole	15	High	Quick
BEETS	Quartered if large; halved if small	9	High	Natural
BROCCOLI	Cut into florets	1	Low	Quick
BRUSSELS SPROUTS	Halved	2	High	Quick
BUTTERNUT SQUASH	Peeled, ½-inch chunks	8	High	Quick
CABBAGE	Sliced	3–4	High	Quick
CARROTS	½- to 1-inch slices	2	High	Quick
CAULIFLOWER	Whole	6	High	Quick
CAULIFLOWER	Cut into florets	1	Low	Quick
GREEN BEANS	Cut in halves or thirds	3	Low	Quick
POTATOES, LARGE RUSSET (FOR MASHING)	Quartered	8	High	Natural for 8 minutes, then quick
POTATOES, RED	Whole if less than 1½ inches across, halved if larger	4	High	Quick
SPAGHETTI SQUASH	Halved lengthwise	7	High	Quick
SWEET POTATOES	Halved lengthwise	8	High	Natural

MEASUREMENT CONVERSIONS

VOLUME EQUIVALENTS	U.S. STANDARD	U.S. STANDARD (OUNCES)	METRIC (APPROXIMATE)
LIQUID	2 tablespoons	1 fl. oz.	30 mL
	¼ cup	2 fl. oz.	60 mL
	½ cup	4 fl. oz.	120 mL
	1 cup	8 fl. oz.	240 mL
	1½ cups	12 fl. oz.	355 mL
	2 cups or 1 pint	16 fl. oz.	475 mL
	4 cups or 1 quart	32 fl. oz.	1 L
	1 gallon	128 fl. oz.	4 L
DRY	⅛ teaspoon	—	0.5 mL
	¼ teaspoon	—	1 mL
	½ teaspoon	—	2 mL
	¾ teaspoon	—	4 mL
	1 teaspoon	—	5 mL
	1 tablespoon	—	15 mL
	¼ cup	—	59 mL
	⅓ cup	—	79 mL
	½ cup	—	118 mL
	⅔ cup	—	156 mL
	¾ cup	—	177 mL
	1 cup	—	235 mL
	2 cups or 1 pint	—	475 mL
	3 cups	—	700 mL
	4 cups or 1 quart	—	1 L
	½ gallon	—	2 L
	1 gallon	—	4 L

OVEN TEMPERATURES

FAHRENHEIT	CELSIUS (APPROXIMATE)
250°F	120°C
300°F	150°C
325°F	165°C
350°F	180°C
375°F	190°C
400°F	200°C
425°F	220°C
450°F	230°C

WEIGHT EQUIVALENTS

U.S. STANDARD	METRIC (APPROXIMATE)
½ ounce	15 g
1 ounce	30 g
2 ounces	60 g
4 ounces	115 g
8 ounces	225 g
12 ounces	340 g
16 ounces or 1 pound	455 g

INDEX

ACKNOWLEDGMENTS

To my husband, Shawn, to whom this book is dedicated. Thanks for putting up with my nonsense, tasting all of my recipes (even when they have tomatoes), and being honest with me even when you know I won't like it.

To everyone who has read my blog, Healthy Delicious, whether you're a devoted fan or just a passerby. I wouldn't do this if it wasn't for your support, enthusiasm, and excitement. Nothing makes me happier than when you tell me one of my recipes is your new favorite.

To the entire blogging community, but especially to the FBE Rockstars for encouraging me to keep going when it all seemed overwhelming. Best. Support. Team. Ever.

To my friends, thank you for your constant support and encouragement. I miss you all so much!

And last but certainly not least, to Ashley Brownell for her assistance developing the recipes for this book. I literally could not have written it without you.

ABOUT THE AUTHOR

Lauren Keating is the author behind the blog *Healthy Delicious*, where she has been sharing easy weeknight recipes made with fresh, nutritious ingredients for over a decade.

Lauren studied plant-based professional cooking through Rouxbe cooking school and uses those skills to incorporate fruits, vegetables, and whole grains into her recipes in unique ways.

Lauren lives in upstate New York with her husband, Shawn, and their two dogs and lives by the motto: If it isn't delicious, it isn't worth eating.

This is Lauren's third cookbook. Get more recipes in her first two books, *Healthy Eating One-Pot Cookbook* and *Healthy Meal Prep Slow Cooker Cookbook,* or at Healthy-Delicious.com. You can also find her on Instagram @HealthyDelish.

CPSIA information can be obtained
at www.ICGtesting.com
Printed in the USA
JSHW041715050721
16602JS00004B/135